Witchitorium

A Glossary of Magic, Witchcraft & Spirituality

Witchitorium

A Glossary of Magic, Witchcraft & Spirituality

Nixie Vale

London, UK
Washington, DC, USA

First published by Moon Books, 2026
Moon Books is an imprint of Collective Ink Ltd.,
Unit 11, Shepperton House, 89 Shepperton Road, London, N1 3DF
office@collectiveinkbooks.com
www.collectiveinkbooks.com
www.moon-books.net

For distributor details and how to order please visit the 'Ordering' section on our website.

ISBN: 978 1 917704 38 0
978 1 917704 43 4 (ebook)
Library of Congress Control Number: 2025935602

A CIP catalogue record for this book is available from the British Library.

Design: Lapiz Digital Services

UK: Printed and bound by CPI Group (UK) Ltd, Croydon, CR0 4YY
US: Printed and bound by Thomson-Shore, 7300 West Joy Road, Dexter, MI 48130

The manufacturer's authorised representative in the EU for product safety is:
eucomply OÜ - Pärnu mnt 139b-14, 11317 Tallinn, Estonia, hello@ eucompliancepartner.com,
www.eucompliancepartner.com

Contents

The mere knowledge of a fact is pale;
but when you come to realize your fact, it takes on color.
Mark Twain

Acknowledgements

I would like to thank each person who has played a part in the production of this book. There are too many to thank here, but I am grateful to each of you. Eva and Kerry for listening to my crazy ideas and supporting me all the way. Luna, for inspiring me to write this book. My production team have been amazing through the entire process. Lastly, I want to thank my ever-suffering partner Beran, who has listened intently, asked questions and pushed me out of my comfort zone.

About the Author

Nixie Vale is the creator of Ramblings of a Rainbow Witch, and while it began as a small Facebook page it has grown over the last thirteen years. She began her spiritual path over 25 years ago, and as she has grown, her path has changed and grown with her. She began her path with researching and learning about Wicca, and it will always have a special place in her heart, but as she grew, she was drawn to other things. She has studied a wide range of subjects from Ancient Egyptian, Ancient Greek, Ancient Norse and Ancient Roman beliefs and practices.

> *Being a Rainbow Witch, to me, means that I will never tire of my spirituality, it will never bore me, and it will never become a burden to me* ~ Nixie Vale

Nixie is a certified crystal healer with the School of Natural Health Sciences. She has studied colour psychology and colour magic extensively and her love of colour and rainbows led to the moniker of Rainbow Witch. She has written over 300 articles, many of which have been published in magazines like Magical Recipes Online, Metaphysical Times, The Spooky Isles as well as others. She is the author of *Wicca: Charms, Potions and Lore*.

Author's Note

I have been on my spiritual journey and a witch for over 25 years, and over the years I have found there are words and terms that I don't know and have had to turn to the internet – or back before the explosion of the internet and Google – the library. While writing this book I have found myself learning so many new things, and I love to learn and expand my knowledge and understanding about my path and the craft that I love.

I hope that you discover a love for the craft and its beauty through reading these pages.

A

Abundance Cheque – The Abundance Cheque is a tool that can be used to create and attract abundance into your life. They are generally used around the New Moon. Sometimes the act of doing ***something*** is all it takes to attract what you need.

Adept – An Adept is someone who has achieved a certain level of knowledge in a single field. An adept is usually initiated into an Occult practice, once they have reached a certain aptitude in relevant schools of knowledge; including magic and alchemy.

Aesir/Æsir – The Aesir are the chief gods of Norse Mythology, and dwell in Asgard. Odin is the leader of the Aesir gods.

Affirmation – The Affirmation is a sentence with powerful words, and always uses positive words. This sentence is aimed to speak to your conscious and unconscious mind to motivate you. They can be extremely helpful for those who lack confidence of self-esteem. The more you say the affirmation, the more your thought patterns can change.

Air – Air is one of the Fundamental elements of nature, along with Earth, Fire and Water. The essence of the Air Element is, transformation, divine connection and the "breath of life".

Air Signs – When someone is born under the Air element, they are said to be thinkers, communicators and like to be doing things. At times they have a 'live and let live' attitude. The signs that are born under the Air element are; Gemini, Libra and Aquarius.

Alchemy – Alchemy is the medieval forerunner to sciences like chemistry, and focused on the transmutation of matter. Alchemists focused on the idea of changing base metals into gold. There is a degree of philosophy to Alchemy, which teaches the art of transformation and change.

Aleister Crowley – A notable character in magical and occult history. He was prominent in early-modern esoteric belief and practice and has remained an influential figure.

Alexandrian Wicca – This is a branch of Wicca that was formed by Alex and Maxine Sanders in the 1960's. Alexandrian Wicca focuses on the polarity and duality of the God and Goddess.

Altar – An altar is a sacred place, where you can gather objects and tools that have a ritual or magical meaning to you. You can use an altar in a number of magical workings, or meditation and study.

Altar Cloth – An altar cloth is a piece of cloth that you use to cover your altar; to protect the surface you are using during rituals and magical work.

Akasha – Akasha represents the interconnectedness of all living things, and is a space where the collective past, and the future exist. It is also considered to be the energy of the conscious and unconscious mind.

Akashic Records – The Akashic Records is a library where all events in the Universe have been recorded. It contains the thoughts, intentions, feelings and words that have occurred, are occurring or may occur in the future.

Amulet – An amulet is a magically charged object which can be used for a plethora of reasons. They are usually associated with protection, luck or healing.

Anatomical Ingredients – These are magical ingredients that come from the body of a person or animal. This could be blood, bones, fur or whiskers. *Depending on the magical intent you are working towards, other things can be required, tears or semen, for example.*

Ancestor – Traditionally, someone who lived before your grandparents. For example, my mum's grandparents are classed as my ancestors because I never knew them. Some consider anyone born before 1900 to be their ancestor.

Angel – Angels are considered to be attendants, agents and messengers of God. Traditionally they are represented as a human with large white wings, a halo and extraordinary beauty, but there are cases where an angels is described as inhuman looking or frightening, with a hundred eyes on their wings.

Angel Numbers – Angel Numbers are a sequence of repeated numbers, which are believed to have spiritual significance, wisdom and insight. They can be a sequence like 111 or 1010.

Animal Guide/Totem – This is an animal that has a spiritual meaning to you and provides guidance and wisdom. An animal totem is the spirit of an animal that you call on or invoke for protection or guardianship. These traditions have come to Pagan and Wiccan circles from Native American Spirituality.

Anima – Anima is the true inner self, or the soul. Carl Gustav Jung used the term in his psychological practices. It can also be used to describe the unconscious part of your mind.

Animism – This is the belief that all creatures, trees, rocks, animals and places have spirit of their own.

Ankh – In Egyptian beliefs the Ankh is a representation of eternal life. It also is believed to represent immortality, death and reincarnation.

Anoint – To anoint something you are rubbing (or placing or pouring) oil as part of a religious or ritual ceremony. Some rituals require you to anoint a candle, tool or even person with a special oil as part of preparations for the ritual.

Anointing Oil – This is a blend of oils which is used for magical, ritual and religious practices.

Anthropomorphic – This means something has human characteristics and traits to non-human beings. Deities such as Anubis and Krishna are considered to be anthropomorphic deities due to their animal forms. In modern media, Mickey Mouse, Goofy and Donald Duck are anthropomorphic creatures because of their ability to talk, and have human thoughts and feelings.

Apparition – An apparition is a ghost-like image of a person, and is an unexpected sight. Apparitions are usually associated with paranormal activity.

Apogee – This is the point at which the Moon (or a satellite) is at the furthest point from Earth.

Apothecary – An apothecary is someone who would make medicines. Today we call these people pharmacists and chemists.

Arcane – Arcane is used to describe something that is only known to a few people, and is considered mysterious and secretive.

Arcana – This describes the two separate groups in a deck of Tarot cards. The Major Arcana describes the twenty-two "trump" cards, and the Minor Arcana describes the fifty-six suit cards.

Archetype – This is a figure or pattern of energy that occurred multiple times throughout history. Archetypes transcend time, place and language but are reflected in the human experience.

Asatru – Asatru means "faith in the Æsir" (Aesir), those who follow the Aesir gods of the Norse/Germanic religion.

Ascension – This is the process of progression to a higher level of consciousness; this is considered to be an innate part of natural evolution of the Spirit.

Ascended Master – Ascended Masters are humans who have become spiritually enlightened, but in past lives were ordinary folk who have gone through a single or a series of transformations of the soul.

Ascendant – This means rising in power, influence or position.

Ascending Node – The Ascending Node is where the Moon moves into the Northern Elliptical Hemisphere. This is also known as the North Node.

Ascending Sign – This is also known as Rising Sign. This is the sign which was on the eastern horizon at the moment of your birth.

Asterism – This is a term that has two definitions, 1) a group or pattern of stars that is not a constellation. 2) a star-shaped reflection and refraction of light on the surface of a crystal, which is formed by microscopic parallel fibres or needle-like inclusions which intersect at the right angle to for the star.

Astral Body – This is part of the Energy field of the body, and is situated between the Mental Body and the Etheric Temple.

Astral Plane – This is a plane of existence between the physical and spiritual realms. While the Astral plane is separate from the Physical plane, it is accessible through certain techniques.

Astral Projection – Astral projection is the process of consciously sending your consciousness from your body to the Astral Plane.

Astrology – Astrology is the study of the planets, Moon, Sun and stars. There is a belief system that surrounds these movements, and how they influence people.

Asperger – Asperger describes the rite of sprinkling a group of people with holy water. While associated with Christianity, some Witches use Moon Water, or other charged water over a gathering, especially at a ritual event.

Athame – Traditionally, an Athame is a black handled, double-sided knife used to inscribe candles, for example, in witchcraft. The Athame is always has a blunt blade, as it is not intended to physically cut anything. Nowadays you can purchase Athames in a plethora of different styles.

Attune – To attune is to bring something into harmony. Attunement is when you intentionally connect more closely to your spiritual self, your source and life current; to become attuned you need to make a conscious.

Aura – Your aura is a luminous, multi-layered shroud that surrounds your body with energy. There are seven layers within the Auric field, and if something is wrong, there may present itself in the physical body.

- The Etheric Body is closest to the physical body, and extends from 0.25 to 2 inches from the body. This layer is associated with the muscles, bones and tissues.
- The Emotional Body is more fluid that the Etheric Body in that it does not fit the physical form, and it extends about 3 inches from the body. This layer associated feelings and emotions.
- The Mental Body is more subtle than the Emotional Body and extends from 3 to 8 inches from the physical body. This layer is associated with the state of mind.
- The Astral Body is the bridge to the spiritual plane, and extended from 6 inches to a foot away from the physical body. This layer is associated with bonds and connections to others.
- The Etheric Temple Body is the template for the body before it is born and extends from 1.5 feet to 2 feet from the body. This layer is associated with the evolution of the individual.
- The Celestial Body is the spiritual emotions and extends from 2 feet to 2.5 feet from the physical body. This layer is associated with spiritual awakenings, and where someone would feel "spiritual ecstasy".
- The Etheric Temple and is the layer that holds all the others. It is the mental level of the spiritual plane. This

layer extends about 3.5 feet from the physical body. This layer is associated with connection to the universe and the divine.

Automatic Writing – Automatic Writing is the process of someone producing written words without consciously writing. This is popular in the paranormal world, where a practitioner channels a spirit or entity to write their words.

Awakening – An awakening is where you have a new awareness of reality and who you truly are. It is common for those who have an awakening to uncover the true meaning and purpose in life.

B

"Baby" Witch – This is a modern term, which is used to describe someone who is new to the craft, or have little experience. Some consider "baby witch" as a slur, or as a way to discredit someone's experience. It has been used prevalently on social media, especially TikTok.

Baculum – This is another name for the penial bone that is present in many mammals, and is primarily used into folk magic like Hoodoo. A penile bone is a bone that is found within the penis of some mammals, including primates, rodents and bats to name a few.

Balefire – A Balefire is a large outdoor fire. They were lit to drive away bad/evil spirits away from a celebration such as Beltane and Samhain.

Baneful Magic – Baneful Magic is a form of magic that has a specific negative intention. It is a term that is used for hexes, jinxes and curses. Unlike most forms of magic, if you have enough anger, rage or strong negative emotion, this can be enough to cast a baneful spell. This is why baneful magic can be so dangerous, because it can be done without conscious thought. If a witch intended to cast a curse, they will be far more focused than something done through unconscious desire.

Banishment – To banish something you are intentionally getting rid of something that is unwanted. It is usually part of preparing an area for spells or rituals. This can also be used to rid yourself of negative or unwanted people.

Baphomet – Baphomet is a symbol of balance in a number of occult and mystical practices. It was the deity the Templars were accused of worshipping, but its modern resurgence comes from The Satanic Temple and the *Satanic Bible* written by Anton LaVey.

Bard – To be a Bard, is to master song and verse and weave magic with them. They are inspired by all things sacred, and share their innate musical talent to weave magic.

Bell – The Bell is used to clear a space of negative, stagnant or weird energy. They are also a way of calling energy to you, especially in rituals.

Black Magic – Much like Baneful Magic, Black Magic is using magic in a way that will harm, or negatively impact another. Historically, Black Magic was believed to be when a witch called on an evil spirit for evil means.

Black Moon – The Black Moon is the inverse of the Blue Moon; being it is the second New Moon in a single calendar month and the fourth New Moon in a season.

Black Salt – Black Salt is made using the ashes of herbs and incense and mixing it with salt. Black Salt is Black Salt is often referred to as Witches Salt, and is primarily in defensive magick such as protection, banishment and warding against curses and hexes, though it is equally effective to cast curses and hexes.

Blessed be – This is a blessing from one person to another, which indicates that you wish, happiness, abundance, health or all-around positive things for another person.

Blessing – A blessing is a prayer, or wish for another to have divine protection and favour. It can also be used as an approval for something.

Beloved Dead – Beloved Dead refers to people and animals that you have personally known in your lifetime, and unlike ancestors, these people/animals had an impact on your life, and their passing has affected you.

Beltane – Beltane is a Celtic festival that is celebrated on or around May 1st and signifies the start of the warmer months, and is believed to be the time when the Earth is at its most fertile. This has led to the belief that Beltane is a fertility festival.

Besom – The Besom is a witch's broom, usually round. Over which a married couple jump during a handfasting ceremony or used to "sweep" away bad energy. It is never used to actually sweep the floor, instead it sweeps negativity away.

Bibliomancy – Bibliomancy is a form of divination which uses a random passage from a book and interpreting its wisdom. The bible is a good example of this.

Binding – A magical binding is a specific type of spell that prevents someone from doing something. A binding spell is designed to control, obstruct or deny. *Famously, witches in Britain cast a binding spell on Adolf Hitler to stop him from invading Britain.*

Bind Rune – A Bind Rune is where you combine two or more Runes for a specific purpose. (You are literally binding the Runes together.) They can become powerful talismans for whatever purpose they were combined. Protection is a very popular purpose for creating Bind Runes.

Birthstones – Birthstones are precious or semi-precious gems and crystals that are associated with the month you were born, or your Zodiac sign.

Blood Magic – Blood Magic is a type of magic where blood is used as a primary ingredient. It is an extremely powerful tool that should not be dabbled in. Many witches believe that blood is not necessary in a spell, but for those who have experience with Blood Magic, it adds an extra dimension and depth to the spell or ritual. There are a number of sanitary and health concerns that comes with the nature of blood. *If you use your own blood in a spell, you are tying that spell to you, and tends to be permanent.*

Blood Moon – There are in fact two meanings for the Blood Moon, 1) it is a non-scientific name for a total Lunar Eclipse, and is name as such due to the reddish hue to the visible Moon. 2) In some cultures, the Blood Moon is the Full Moon in October, as this is the time where animals are hunted and their meat prepared for the winter months.

Blood of the Moon – This refers to a woman's menstrual cycle and her period. If a woman's cycle falls on a New Moon it is known as a White Moon Cycle, and if it falls on a Full Moon it is known as a Red Moon Cycle.

Blue Moon – The Blue Moon is the opposite of a Black Moon. The Blue Moon is where there are two Full Moons in a single calendar month, or the fourth Full Moon in a season.

Boline – A Boline is traditionally a white-handled crescent shaped blade used for cutting herbs. Unlike the Athame, the Boline's blade is always sharp, so care should always be taken when using one. A Boline doesn't necessarily have to have a white handle, as ones made with antler or wood have become popular.

Bones – Bones and other animal materials act as effigies (*a sculpture or model of a person or animal)* or a fetish (*representations of the animal and its spirit)*. These objects then tap into the energy of the living animal, and the Spirit of the animal; it will facilitate communication between you and the Spirit, and it can even help you reach back to the energy of your ancestors, protecting you through all kinds of ancestral work.

Book of Mirrors – A Book of Mirrors is a book where you write your own experiences from an emotional perspective, and becomes a log of your own spiritual journey.

Book of Shadows – A Book of Shadows is a book where a witch keeps information about spells, rituals, prayers, thoughts and any lesson you have learned. You do not need a special book, a notepad or a ring binder will work as a Book of Shadows.

Burning Times – This is a term that refers to the witch trials that occurred from the Dark Ages to the early modern period. Though not all witches were burned, it has become a popular phrase referring to the trials across Europe and American colonies.

C

Call "to" – To Call is when you are attempting to communicate with the Divine, Spirits and other non-corporeal beings.

Candle – A candle is a pillar, taper, or other shape made from wax or tallow with a central wick, which produces a flame as it burns.

Candle Magic – Lighting a candle of different colours and shapes can help manifest your desires. Different colours have different meanings. Pink is associated with love, Green is associated with abundance, and if you make candles the shape and form you create can add another aspect to your spell craft.

Candlemas – Candlemas marks the return of the light, and has become associated with the Pagan festival of Imbolc, which symbolises the halfway point between the Winter Solstice and the Spring Equinox. There is no relation between the celebrations besides where they fall in the calendar.

Cardinal Sign – Cardinal Signs are part of Astrology, and relate to Aries, Cancer, Libra and Capricorn, and they display a degree of restlessness, motivation, ambition and usually become leaders in their communities, the Cardinal Signs are at the beginning of each season. The word Cardinal means chief, primary and principal.

Cardinal Directions – This described the four points of a compass, and are aligned with the rising and setting of the sun. Each point of the compass has their own spiritual meaning.

- **North** – North is associated with the element Earth, and is connected to the hearth, home, security and fertility.
- **South** – South is associated with the element of Fire and is connected to energy, passion, creativity and drive.
- **East** – East is associated with the element of Air, and connected to communication, new beginnings, growth and expansion. East is where the Sun rises so it has been seen as the birthplace of the gods.
- **West** – West is associated with the element of Water, and is connected to the psyche, emotions and movement. West is where the Sun sets and has been associated with endings, often where the dead were once buried.

Cartomancy – This is a form of divination which people interpret the meaning of a random selection of cards. Unlike tarot, a Cartomancy deck has 54 cards (52 cards and 2 joker cards.) If you are familiar with tarot, the meanings of the suits can relate, for example, the suit of Hearts relate to the suit of Cups.

Celestial – Celestial has many meanings in the Spiritual world.

1. The visible sky or outer space, which can be observed.
2. Pertaining to Heaven or heavenly spaces where deities or the dead reside.

Celestial Equator – The Celestial Equator is an imaginary celestial line that lies over the actual equator. The Equinoxes occur when the Sun crosses this point, meaning that the hours of night and day are equal. The dates of the Equinoxes depend on when the Sun passes over this imaginary line.

Centring – The term centring is a process of focusing on the energy at the centre of your body. Traditionally you pair centring with the process of grounding as a prelude to performing spells and rituals.

Censer – The Censer is a container where incense is burned during rituals, ceremonies and meditation.

Ceremonial Clothing – This is a special set of clothing that you use in your magical working. This can include a cloak and robe, but it doesn't need to be.

Ceremonial Magic – Ceremonial Magic is also known as High Magic, and is a wide variety of magic which a number of accessories are required. Ceremonial Magic draws from a number of philosophical schools of thought such as Hermetic Qabalah, Thelema and Esoterica.

Chakra – The word Chakra comes from the Sanskrit word for "wheel" and refers to energy centres in the body. These points of the body are thought to be spinning wheels/disks of energy, that flow from one to another. A Chakra can be open and closed, but it is possible for a Chakra to be "too" open as well. If the chakras are out of balance, it may have an effect on the mental, emotional, physical and spiritual self.

- The Base/Root Chakra is located at the base of the spine and is represented by the colour red. This Chakra is associated with survival, practicality, materialism, and physical needs.
- The Sacral Chakra is located in the lower abdomen and is represented by the colour orange. This Chakra is associated with creativity, emotions, sexual drive and sexuality.
- The Solar Plexus Chakra is located just below the ribcage, close to the navel and is represented by the colour yellow.

This Chakra is associated with confidence, personal power, the identity of self.

- The Heart Chakra is located at the centre of the chest and is represented with the colour green (it can also be represented by the colour pink). This Chakra is associated with love, relationships, sharing, and personal development.
- The Throat Chakra is located at the throat and is represented by the colour blue. This Chakra is associated with expression, communication and the flow of information.
- The Brow/Third Eye Chakra is located in the centre of your eyebrows and is represented by the colour indigo. This Chakra is associated with intuition, knowledge, psychic abilities and perception.
- The Crown Chakra is located at the top of your head and is represented by the colour violet. This Chakra is associated with inspiration, spirituality and being at one with the universe.

Charm – A Charm is a magical spell, or an object that is designed to bring you luck. The four-leaf clover can be considered a good luck charm, so can a horseshoe.

Chalice – A Chalice is a cup, glass or even a bowl that serves as a representation of the feminine energies of the Universe, it is also used as a representation for the element of Water. In symbolic versions of the Great Rite, the Chalice represents the Goddess. When not used in the Great Rite, a chalice may contain wine or water and passed around a group/coven to be sipped as part of a ritual.

Changeling – A Changeling is a child that has been secretly swapped for a Fae child. One sign that a child may be a

Changeling is by how they grow; if they are smaller and sicklier than a human child.

Channelling – When you are channelling energy you become the conductive conduit between a source of energy and an energy sink, where energy is absorbed or dissipated. Much like an electrical cable and a lamp. You plug one end into the socket (the source of energy) and the lamp (what requires energy). However, unlike the lamp and cable, you have an energy source within you, it's your spiritual energy.

Chanting – Literally, a chant is the repetition of a single word or phrase. The words used in the chant are believed to have magical, mystical or a special power.

Charge of the Goddess/God – This is a Wiccan texts which is designed to be inspirational, and recited is Wiccan Rituals.

Charge "to" – When you charge something you are imbuing it with a specific kind of energy. You can charge your crystals under the Full Moon. You can charge your morning beverage – tea or coffee – with positive energy by stirring clockwise saying "fill my day with positive light" then drinking as usual.

Chatoyancy – This is used to described an optical effect of a crystal that as a reflectance similar to a cats' eye. Tiger's eye is a perfect example of Chatoyancy.

Chi – In Chinese philosophy Chi is the energy that is believed to be inherent in all things, and a balance in the Chi (also known as Ki or Qi) is vital for good health and wellbeing.

Chinese Astrology – Chinese Astrology is a zodiac system based on animal signs which have a 12-year cycle. Each animal has characteristics which are said to be bestowed when you are born. The animals include; Rat, Pig, Monkey, Snake and Horse to name a few.

Chromotherapy – This is a method of healing that uses the visible light spectrum to treat and cure illnesses, and manage a range of different types of pain.

Circle – A Magic circle is a space which is drawn out or marked by a practitioner for the use in rituals and spells. A circle is usually a cleansed space in which you will do your magical work, and is created as a form of protection against unwanted external energy.

Clairaudience – Clairaudience is the ability to hear something that is not present to the physical auditory system. This is associated with the paranormal field and spiritual readers, such as mediums and tarot readers.

Claircognizance – Claircognizance is the ability to know something that you have not learned about, and has no logical explanation.

Clairsentience – Clairsentience is the ability to perceive and feel psychic energy. This is most associated with the paranormal field, mediumship and readers.

Clairvoyance – Clairvoyance is the ability to see things that are not perceived by others. This is most associated with the paranormal field, mediumship and readers

Classical Planets – The Classical Planets refer to Saturn, Jupiter, Mars, the Sun, Venus, Mercury and the Moon. The list excludes Uranus, Neptune and Pluto. The sequence goes from slowest planet to the fastest moving planet in the night sky, and the rulership of the hours of the day are in this order too.

Cleansing – Cleansing is the act of removing negative or unwanted energy from a space, an object or the body. When you cleanse something, you are returning it to its original, baseline state.

Closed Practice – A Closed Practice refers to any practice that someone needs to be born into or have been through an initiation process which requires learning about the practice. Smudging is an indigenous practice that is considered closed as there is more to the practice than burning sacred herbs.

Collective Consciousness – This describes the belief that people share a greater connection, which unifies them through experiences and beliefs.

Collective Reading – A Collective Reading is a reading done for general purposes, as it is not designed to for one person. Collective Readings can give information on energy that is around us at that moment.

Colour Magic – Colour Magic is using the colours of the visible spectrum to set a specific intention, or invoke a certain type of energy.

Cone of Power – When a witch (or a group) gathers, raises and generates energy, in a circle which takes the form of a cone. This is often done in Wicca during rituals through the movement of their bodies and the words they chant.

Consecration – This is the act of making something sacred, and while the declaration of something being sacred may be enough for some, there is often more to it as it can require cleansing, purification and dedication for sacred purposes.

Contemplation – Contemplation is the practice of deep reflective thought.

Conjuration – This is a magical incantation, chant or spell that brings something into being.

Cord Cutting – Cord Cutting is the practice of severing physical, mental, emotional and spiritual ties with someone or something that is no longer good for you.

Corn Dolly – A Corn Dolly is made during the harvest season, usually from the last sheaf of corn cut. Today it may not be possible to know it is the last, so it is made from sheafs of corn. It was believed that the Spirit of Grain inhabits the doll and would be reborn through the act of making the doll.

Cornucopia – A cornucopia is traditionally a horn shaped vessel that is usually filled with fruits and vegetables, grains and flowers. It is believed to have originated in Greece and Rome roughly 3,000 years ago.

Correspondences – Correspondences are based on the belief that you can influence something through its relation to something else, especially with plants, fruits, vegetables, and crystals to name a few.

Cosmic Energy – Cosmic energy is defined as an energy source that is external to the body. In other cultures, it is called Prana, Kundalini and Shakti.

Cosmos – The Cosmos refers to the Universe, and all the various bodies within it. It has been used to refer to an ordered universe which is in harmony.

Coven – A Coven is a gathering, group or community of like-minded witches.

Covenstead – A Covenstead is a place where a group, or coven of witches gather. This is a regular meeting place, but it doesn't need to be a brick-and-mortar building, but is usually the home of a member of the coven itself.

Craft "the" – The Craft is a shortened version of Witchcraft and it is often used instead. For example, "my favourite aspect of the craft is…." It is also the name of an influential 1996 film about a group of four girls practicing the craft.

Crescent – This describes the curved, sickle shape of the Moon during the Waxing and Waning phases.

Crone – A Crone is a woman that is in the later years of her life, and is the third aspect of the Triple Goddess. She is the culmination of wisdom, experience and shares her knowledge with others in her community.

Crossroads – The crossroads is a place where different roads meet and separate, and is believed to be a place where two worlds meet. There are three types of crossroads.

1. T shaped cross roads are considered to be masculine, and are believed to be the best place to work with masculine energy.
2. X shaped crossroads are considered to be feminine and the best place to work with feminine energy.

3. Y shaped crossroads are considered to be places where you can interact with the Divine, or the Fae, for example.

Crossroads Dirt – This is soil collected at a specific type of crossroads for the magical work you are wanting to do.

Crystal – A piece of naturally forming rock that has natural geometrically regular atomic structure. In the metaphysical world, a crystal is a precious or semi-precious stone that can be used for healing, crafting or decoration.

Crystal Grid – A Crystal Grid is a collection of crystals that are placed in specific positions to create patterns which will mirror and enhance your intentions.

Crystal Healing – Crystal Healing is a non-invasive form of healing using vibrational frequencies and energy to heal a range of things from the mental and emotional to the physical and spiritual.

Crystal Magic – Crystal Magic is a form of magic where a witch uses crystals to amplify or attract energy. Crystals can be used as amulets, charms, talismans, and for divinatory purposes.

Cult – This is used to describe a small religious group that isn't affiliated with any religion or religious movement. The members tend to hold strict or extreme views which are considered dangerous. While not directly associated with Witchcraft, over the years magical practices have been seen as cult-like.

Cunning Folk – Cunning Folk refers to people who practiced folk medicine like herbal remedies, healing for common ailments, and midwifery. Sometimes Cunning Folk were accused of witchcraft, but the primary distinction was they used their skill to heal, protect and help others, rather than doing harm. It is also believed that Cunning men and women would try to combat the evil and malicious magic performed by "witches". This is a term used during the Middle Ages.

Curse – This is a kind of spell that is used to bring misfortune to another. It is also a term that is used to describe an utterance of a deity which is to inflict harm to someone or as punishment. *Athena cursed Arachne to the form of a spider because of how she depicted the gods in her tapestry. Athena also cursed Medusa to be a Gorgon after she was "defiled" by Poseidon.*

D

Daemon – This is an older way of spelling Demon, and comes from Ancient Greece. It was also used to describe a divine or supernatural being, that had no moral alignment.

Dagger – A Dagger is a short knife with a pointed, edged blade. They can be blunted and used as athames to direct energy.

Dedication – This is the act of committing yourself to something meaningful, and the acquisition of knowledge and skills. Some covens have a dedication ritual, and those that do have this as part of joining the group.

Deity – From a Polytheistic view, it refers to any god or goddess, while from a Monotheistic view, it refers to the creator God.

Déjà Vu – Déjà Vu is the feeling that you have already experienced something before, but the reality being you haven't experienced it. Déjà Vu can be translated to "already seen" indicating that feeling of living an identical moment before.

Demon – A Demon is an evil spirit, devil or entity that acts as a tormentor, and is considered to be evil and cruel.

Demonology – Demonology is the study of demons from religions, mythologies and cultures from around the world.

Demon Trap Jar – While this sounds ominous, it simply refers to a jar that has been filled with increasingly smaller stones. You place in pebbles, stone chips and sand until the jar is completely full and there is no space in the jar. Place the jar at your front door, saying something like "no evil can enter without counting what's in the jar". The belief is that the evil entity/spirit/demon has to count every single grain in the jar, which prevents them from entering.

Deosil – Deosil describes the movement of going to the right, clockwise or in the direction of the sun.

Descending Node – The Descending Node is where the Moon enters the Southern Elliptical Hemisphere, and is also known as the South Node.

Discernment – This is the action of taking all information into account before making a decision or judgement about something.

Distance Healing – Distance Healing is as it describes; healing someone or something at a distance. It requires the transfer energy from the practitioner, to the intended target. Reiki is an example of how healing can be done without needing to touch the recipient.

Divination – Divination is the art and practice of seeking knowledge, wisdom and information concerning the future through supernatural means. Tarot and Runes are both forms of divination.

Divine – Divine means that someone or something has the qualities, and characteristics of a god, goddess or deity.

Divine Feminine – This is a concept that symbolises qualities, characteristics and attributes associated with femininity. It is believed to give birth to all life which has been seeded.

Divine Masculine – This is a concept that symbolises qualities, characteristics and attributes associated with masculinity. It is believed to be the seed from which all life is formed.

Divinity – This is the quality or state of a divine being. Gods, Goddesses as well as other spiritual entities are considered to be part of Divinity.

Doppelganger – When someone who looks freakishly similar to you, but isn't a twin or relation. They are often seen as omens of bad luck or misfortune.

Dowsing – Dowsing is the act of using a forked piece of wood (Hazel, Rowan or Willow work best) or a Y shaped metal instrument to find hidden water sources, deceased bodies or anything that needs to be found.

Drawing Down the Moon – Drawing Down the Moon is a beautiful and powerful ritual where a witch calls upon the Divine – the Goddess – and invites them directly into themselves.

Drawing Down the Sun – Drawing Down the Sun is a beautiful and powerful ritual where a witch calls upon the Divine – the God – and invites them directly into themselves.

Dreamwork – Dreamwork is anything related to paying attention to and the interpretation of dreams, which can teach us something new about ourselves.

Dream Analysis – Dream Analysis is a part of dreamwork, and searches for the meanings behind our dreams, and how the meanings can help us grow.

Dressing Oil – This is an oil that is used to anoint candles and other objects used in rituals.

Dressing a Candle – When you dress a candle you are adding herbs to the surface of the candle, which are associated to the intention and focus of your spell.

Druid – A Druid is a priest(ess), magician, soothsayer of the Celtic religion, and in modern times a Druid is someone who follows a path derived from the Celtic religion.

Druidry – Druidry is a religious movement and spiritual practice based on old Celtic beliefs and have a focus on the Earth and nature worship.

Druzy – This refers to a thin layer of sparkling crystalline structures on the surface of a rock or crystal.

Dualism – This is the belief that things are divided into two contrasting or opposing parts. The struggles between good and evil in Zoroastrianism is a good example of Dualism, and for some the equal belief in God and the Devil as opposing forces are also an example of Dualism.

Duo theism – In Wicca the belief in the god and goddess is considered to be a good example of Duo Theism.

E

Earth – One of the four fundamental elements of nature, along with Air, Water and Fire. It is what provides our connection to the physical world. Earth is also the name of the orb that we live on, and it's this connection to the physical world that is represented by Earth.

Earth Sign – When someone is born under the Earth element, they are said to be pragmatic, reliable, logical and has a strong connection to the physical world. These people tend to have an unwavering determination. Those born under the Earth sign are; Taurus, Virgo and Capricorn.

Earthing – Earthing is another name for Grounding, which is the process of standing directly on natural earth – grass, soil, sand etc – so you can release any unwanted or negative energy. This is usually done periodically, but is suggested to be done before any form of magical or spiritual work.

Earth Magic – This is a form of magic that uses nature and elements from the Earth in spells and magical working. Sticks, stones, soil and even water all fall under the Earth Magic banner.

Effigy – An Effigy is a roughly made, humanoid model that is created into order to be destroyed or damaged. This has become a form of protest, but it can also be used in hexes, jinxes and curses.

Egg – The Egg is a symbol of fertility, new life and rebirth. They are a popular symbol around Ostara and Easter.

Egregore – An Egregore is an entity or thought form that has been created by a group who have strong beliefs, intention, feelings and goals. This creates a powerful energy field and can be used for anything from protection to destruction.

Elemental – An Elemental is a being or supernatural entity that is associated with one of the four natural elements. A Salamander is an example of a fire elemental.

(The) Elements – The classical elements refer to Earth, Air, Fire, Water (and eventually Spirit would be added) which were once believed to explain nature, and all matter. Earth refers to stability and structure. Air represents movement and expansion. Fire represents energy and lifeforce. Water represents flexibility and adaptability.

Elixir – An Elixir is a magical or medicinal concoction or potion which was created for a specific purpose. In Alchemy it is believed to be a substance that could turn base metals into gold.

Empath – An empath is someone that that is believed to have the ability to feel and perceive what other people and animals feel and experience. They intuitively experience the whole spectrum of emotion, good and bad.

Empathy – Empathy is the ability to understand and experience the feelings, urges and even thoughts of others. We call these people Empaths.

Enchant – To enchant someone is to use magic to cast a spell over them.

Enchantment – An enchantment is a spell, charm or incantation which is intended to trigger a magical effect on a person or an object. Enchantments have been known to be sung or chanted while being performed.

Energy Work – This describes anything a witch or a spiritual person does with their energy, and how they work with external energy as well. Spell work is a form of energy handling, and Reiki healing is another, different form of energy handling.

Enlightenment – This is the process of gaining awareness, knowledge, wisdom and understanding which brings clarity and purpose to a person's life.

Entity – An entity is a single thing that has a separate and distinct experience of the world. In a spiritual sense, an entity is an immaterial being that include angels, ghosts and folkloric characters such as fairies. Oftentimes, the entity can be abstract and not fit into a descriptive box.

Equinox – Each year there are two Equinoxes, which occur when the Sun passes the celestial equator. It's a time when night and day are at equal length. They occur around the 21st of March and 21st September, but the dates and times vary from year to year.

Esoteric – Something that is Esoteric in nature is likely only to be understood by a few people, or by people who have a specialised subset of knowledge.

Essential Oils – Essential Oils are oils which have been through a pressing or distillation process and have the odour and taste that is characteristic of the plant.

Ether – Ether is an element that is considered to make all life possible. It means "space" which is both something and nothing all at the same time. It has been described as stillness, yet it makes all movement possible.

Ethics – Moral principles that dictates a person's behaviour and actions. The Wiccan Rede is an example of a moral code of ethics, which boils down to don't do any harm or there will be consequences.

Evil Eye – The Evil Eye is a curse that originated in the culture of ancient Greece that was believed to cause harm to the target. It was usually related to things like envy and jealousy, and would bring bad luck to the target.

Evocation – Evocation is often misused and mixed up with Invocation, but in generally when you are doing an evocation, you are inviting a god or goddess into your circle, but you do not invite them into your body. An example of evocation is when you call the quarters to attend, protect and act as guardians of your magical work.

Exorcism – This is the act and spiritual practice of expelling a demon, djinn, or other spiritual entity that has entered someone without permission. Exorcisms are generally only considered by monotheistic religions like Christianity.

F

Faerie – The Fae is a category of mythical or supernatural creature which inhabit the world, but are unseen by people for the most part. Faeries, the Fae, fair folk and fairies are just some of the names these beings are known by and how they appear depends on where you live, and the folklore of the region. The Fae are generally anthropomorphic in nature, and may even be considered as teeny-tiny people. The term Fae is used to refer to beings like Gnomes, Pixies, Elves, Sprites. Like their human counter parts, some Fae are benevolent, helpful and even kind, while others are tricksters, cruel and have a general malevolence about them. The regions of the UK have a rich depth of faerie folklore. In Scotland, there are two distinct groups of Fae, the Seelie and Unseelie courts.

- The Seelie Court are neutral beings that either helped humans, or at least stay neutral in nature.
- The Unseelie Court are chaotic, mischievous, impulsive and wild. They will play tricks on humans, and even go as far as harming humans.

Faerie Burgh – In Scotland, a Faerie Burgh is a mound of earth that covers an underground colony of Faeries.

Fairy – We are most familiar with "Fairy" being benevolent beings that help and protect humans in children's stories. Tinkerbell and the Blue Fairy from Pinocchio are examples of this type of fairy.

Faith – Faith is all about belief and whether it is religious or spiritual, and does not require any kind of proof to have confidence and trust. Faith is a deep and abiding trust in someone or something, and you need no proof of their power, ability or existence. During difficult times, faith can provide hope, meaning, solace and strength. Depending on what you have faith in, it could mean submission to doctrine, or it could mean a commitment to a set of teachings.

Familiar – Depending on where you look for the definition, in the Middle Ages a familiar was a spirit or demon which was called to do a witch's bidding. In the modern world there are two popular definitions 1) a familiar is a Spirit that protects a witch from spiritual harm. 2) An animal that a witch has a deep and spiritual bond with. *I have stived to differentiate between the two modern interpretations, because no witch worth her salt would ever want their pet to be in the path of danger.*

Fates – The Fates are a group of three women in Greek Mythology, they were also known as the Moirai. These women were said to preside over the birth, life and death of both gods and mortals alike, and it's believed they assigned everyone's fate at the moment of their birth. Clotho, known as the Spinner spun the thread of life. Lakhesis measured how long the life would be. Atropos would cut the cord at the time of someone's death.

Feather – A feather grows from a bird's skin to create its plumage, and in witchcraft they represent the element of Air – even if the bird is unable to fly. The bird the feather came from and its colour can have deep and spiritual meanings. Seeing a white feather, seemingly from nowhere is believed to be a loved one that's passed is nearby.

Feng Shui – Feng Shui is a Chinese system of belief that the placement, orientation and spatial arrangements of household items and furniture is needed to ensure a good flow of energy, or Chi. If the Chi is not correct, or there isn't balance of Yin and Yang, then your home and office maybe unbalanced.

Fire – One of the four fundamental elements of nature, along with Air, Water and Earth. It is what provides our connection to the physical world.

Fire Sign – When someone is born under the Fire element, they are said to be bold, energetic, assertive and spontaneous. These people tend to be natural leaders, they are the ones to blaze a trail of their own making. The Fire signs are Aries, Leo and Sagittarius.

Fixed Sign – Fixed signs refer to Taurus, Leo, Scorpio and Aquarius. The role of a Fixed Sign is to maintain and uphold any responsibilities, goals and desires in everyday life. Those born as a Fixed Sign do not welcome change easily, and their role in the Zodiac is to preserve traditions and beliefs. The Fixed Signs represent the middle of seasons, where seasonal stability is achieved.

Florida Water – Florida Water is a Cologne with a citrus scent. In Witchcraft it is used to cleanse energy and provide protection from spaces, tools and the body. It has historically been used in South America during religious and spiritual ceremonies.

Flowers – Spiritually, different flowers have a variety of meanings. This became very popular in the Victorian period with the inception of The Language of Flowers, a technique called Floriography.

Flower of Life – The Flower of Life is a series of overlapping circles that can radiate out infinitely. It holds within it all patterns of Sacred Geometry like the Merkaba and Metatron's

Cube. It represents the creation of all things, and the unity of everything in the universe.

Folklore – Folklore is a set of traditional beliefs and customs that have been handed down from generation to generation through stories. These tend to be shared by word of mouth, and like Chinese Whispers they may change over the generations.

Folk Tales – These are the stories which were shared among generations which held wisdom from past generations.

Foraging – The literal meaning is a person or animal that searches far and wide for food. Today, it has become popular to search for naturally wild and safe food to eat. Some believe that it is safer and free of modern preservation and packaging techniques.

Fossil – A Fossil is the literal remains or the impression of a plant or animal that has become embedded in rock, and become petrified. An Ammonite is an example of a fossilized cephalopod, which lived during the Jurassic and Cretaceous periods.

Free Will – Free Will is an important concept in witchcraft, as it is the literal power of acting without the control of others. When you cast a spell on someone, you always have to take their free will into account. *If you cast a love spell on someone and they fell madly in love with you, you do this by superimposing your will (the spell) over theirs.*

Freezer Spell – A Freezer Spell is a spell that is designed to be put in the freezer in order to prevent someone from doing something. You can keep adversaries at bay, freeze people out of your life, or stop someone from continuing particular behaviours. It is very similar to a binding spell, but you put it in the freezer.

Frequency – In scientific terms, Frequency means the number of waves that pass a certain point in a minute. Frequencies can be used in terms of visible light and sound waves.

Fumigant – This is generally associated with pests and the extermination of such pests, but in the world of witchcraft, a fumigant is referred to the smoke in cleansing as you are essentially getting rid of unwanted or negative energy.

Futhark Runes – The Elder Futhark Runes and Younger Futhark Runes are proto-Norse writing systems that consists of 24 characters or Runes. They were primarily used for writing but over the centuries each figure has been associated with meanings and have been used as a form of divination for a long time. Here is a quick rundown of each Rune both the positive and negative to each rune.

Fehu

- ✓ Money, Hope, Luck, Success and Happiness
- ✓ Failure and Loss

Uruz

- ✓ Physical Strength, Speed and Sexual desire
- ✓ Frailty, Violence and Lust

Thurisaz

- ✓ Self-Discipline, Study and Meditation
- ✓ Compulsion, Evil and Hate

Ansuz

- ✓ Vision, Leadership and Power of Words
- ✓ Delusion, Vanity and Boredom

Raido

- ✓ Travel, Relocation, and the Dance of Life
- ✓ Crisis, Rigidity, Injustice and Death

Kenaz

- ✓ Creativity, Inspiration, Revelation and Knowledge
- ✗ False Hope and No Creativity

Gebo

- ✓ Gifts and Personal Relationships
- ✗ Greed, Obligation and Loneliness

Wunjo

- ✓ Joy, Comfort, Fellowship, Pleasure and Glory
- ✗ Sorrow, Strife and Frenzy

Hagalaz

- ✓ Wrath of Nature, Trials, Tests and Destruction
- ✗ Catastrophe, Loss, Sickness, Hardship and Pain

Nauthiz

- ✓ Endurance, Survival, Determination, and Patience
- ✗ Distress, Need, Drudgery and Restlessness

Isa

- ✓ Challenge and Reinforcement
- ✗ Ego-Mania, Blindness, Deceit, Illusion and Betrayal

Jera/Jara

- ✓ Peace, Happiness, Hope, Earlier Efforts Realised
- ✗ Setbacks, Conflict, Bad Timing and Poverty

Ehwaz

- ✓ Defence, Trustworthiness, Protection and Motivation
- ✗ Confusion, Destruction and Fallibility

Perth

- ✓ Mystery, Hidden Things, Uncertain Meanings
- ✗ Addiction, Malaise, Loneliness

Algiz

- ✓ Protection, Shield, Warding off Evil, Guardian
- ✗ Hidden Danger, Taboo and Warning

Sowilo

- ✓ Life Force, Health, Victory, Honour and Success
- ✗ Bad Counsil, Wrath of God, and Gullibility

Teiwaz

- ✓ Justice, Authority, Analysis and Rationality
- ✗ Strife, War, Stupidity and Dullness

Berkana

- ✓ Birth, Fertility, Growth, Liberation and Love Affair
- ✗ Deceit, Abandon and Loss of Control

Ehwaz

- ✓ Transformation and Sending Communication
- ✗ Reckless, Hassle, Disharmony, Mistrust and Betrayal

Mannaz

- ✓ The Self, Humanity, Social Order and awareness
- ✗ Depression, Slyness, Mortality and Manipulation

Laguz

- ✓ Water, Life, Energy, Dreams and Imagination
- ✗ Confusion, Despair, Suicide and Madness

Inguz

- ✓ Common Sense, Caring, Family, Love, Home and Relief
- ✗ Impotence, Foul, Productions and Work

Dagaz

- ✓ Breakthrough, Planning, Awareness and Awakening
- ✗ Ending, Limit, Contemplation, Hopelessness

Othala

- ✓ Inherited, Prosperity, Group Order and Experience
- ✗ Slippery, Bad Karma and Homelessness

G

Gaia – Gaia is a Greek primordial goddess of Earth. She is believed to be the personification of Earth, and from her all life is born, and to whom all life returns.

Gardnerian Wicca – Gardnerian Wicca is a branch of Wicca that was established by Gerald Gardner whose members today follow his teachings. Some trace their part of the tradition to initiated members of his original members.

Gemstone – A gemstone is a mineral that is prized for its rarity, beauty or durability. Diamond, Sapphire, Emerald and Ruby are the most well-known gemstones, but Alexandrite, Tanzanite, Topaz and Opal are often considered to be gems due to their rarity.

Generational Curse – This is a term that isn't used too much in the witchy world, but a generational curse is where the beliefs and actions of one's ancestors still has an effect on the present day. For those who have a deep spirituality, they may feel that the actions of their ancestors, still hold negative repercussions to this day and that they must atone in some way.

Geomancy – Geomancy is a type of divination that requires handfuls of dirt or earth which is then thrown in the air. How the dirt falls to the ground provides advice and wisdom. In literal terms it means divination with the earth.

Gerald Gardner – Gerald Gardner is considered to be the father of modern witchcraft, and was the founder of Wicca in the 1950's. He has written literary works which are still used today in Gardnerian Wicca as well as solitary witches all over the world.

Ghost – While many things can be considered a "ghost" the general meaning is an apparition of someone (even pets) that has passed away. How they appear may differ from a mass shifting mist or a clear image of the deceased.

Glade – A glade is an open space within a wood or forest.

Glamour Magic – Glamour Magic is a form of enchantment that changes your outwards appearance; however, in reality it's about empowering yourself by choosing what you wear, the clothes, accessories and even cosmetics, and once chosen you imbue them with magic for things life confidence, protection and luck.

God – A male deity.

Goddess – A female deity.

Goetia – This is a type of European magic or witchcraft, and focuses on invoking or calling on angels and other spirits to help with magical workings. Historically it has been associated with demons and evil spirits.

Gnome – A Gnome is a small dwarf-like creature (usually male) with a long beard and a pointed hat. They are said to live underground or in hedgerows, and guard the nearby plant life. It is also said that to have a Gnome in your garden can make it flourish.

Gnostic – Gnostic is a term that relates to knowledge, specifically esoteric and spiritual knowledge and wisdom. Some Gnostics believe that to gain true and genuine knowledge and wisdom is to turn away from the materialism of the modern world and return to live in connection with the Earth and its cycles.

Grave Dirt – Grave Dirt has been a contested term over the years as some believe that it is the dust, dirt and debris that accumulates on gravestones, while others believe that it is the soil that is taken from the top of a person's grave. One thing to keep in mind is when taking the soil from anyone's grave, would they consent to help you with your workings?

Graveyard Dirt – Graveyard Dirt is soil taken from the graveyard itself, not from anyone's grave, but from the outer edges, or the space along walkways and buildings. *Whether you are collecting Grave or Graveyard Dirt you need to give something to appease the Gate Keeper and the spirits within. Coins, crystals, herbs, or flowers, for example. This shows your appreciation for the items taken, and how you are not taking the energy for granted.*

Greater Sabbat – The Greater Sabbats mark an important turning point in the seasons, they are believed to have coincided with days people would be required to pay rent to landlords. Today, witches see them as the markers for seasonal changes.

- Imbolc is the midpoint between Yule and Ostara, and is considered to be the time where you see the first signs of spring.
- Beltane is the mid-point between Ostara and Litha and is considered to be the time of year where the weather stabilises and improves.
- Lughnasadh is the mid-point between Litha and Mabon and is the first of the harvest festivals and is considered to be the time where you see the first signs of Autumn.
- Samhain is the mid-point between Mabon and Yule and is the last of the harvest festivals, usually associated with hunting, slaughter and preparation of animals for the winter months. This is also the time when you can feel a distinct chill of the approaching winter.

Green Man – The Green Man is a figure in Paganism that is associated with rebirth and new growth. The Green Man is a symbol associated with the Horned God, which is an amalgam of Cernunnos and Pan among others.

Green Witch – A Green Witch is someone that works very closely with nature, it's cycles and tools that come directly from nature.

Grey Witch – A Grey Witch is someone that practices witchcraft and is fully aware and embrace the duality of magic. They do not see "white" or "black" magic or good and bad. They accept and celebrate it all.

Grimoire – A Grimoire is a book that contains a witch's spells, rituals and invocations. It is a term that is used interchangeably with Book of Shadows.

Grounding – Grounding is the transfer of excess energy to the earth, and it is this reason that some people refer to it as Earthing. When you are doing spell work, or any kind of energy work, having a connection – whether it's energetically or physically – allows any excess energy to be bled to the Earth and away from your own energy centre. By grounding you are protecting yourself. If you feel agitated, lethargic or disorientated, this can be an indication that you need to ground yourself.

Grove – A Grove in witchcraft can have two meanings, but the most well-known is a small wooded area or a group of trees. Another meaning is a study group of witches which may be led by an established coven. Those in the Grove are not initiated into the coven, as the Grove is for those new to the craft and learning.

Guardian Angel – A Guardian Angel is a spirit that is believed to watch over and protect someone. While some would consider a guardian angel to be an angel, some believe that a deceased relative, animal or mythological figure is their guardian angel. this isn't always the case.

Guru – Traditionally a Guru is a Hindu spiritual teacher and guide, but it is often taken out of the Hindu context today, and is usually refers to someone who is an expert or influential in their area of expertise, but this can be seen as diminishing the role of the true the Hindu spiritual teachers.

H

Hades – Hades is the name of the Greek god of the Underworld, but it is also the name of the underground realm of the dead. This realm is made of three distinct areas. The Asphodel Meadows is where the majority of souls will reside after death. Elysian Fields (Elysium) is a utopian paradise where the spirits of heroes reside. Then there is Tartarus, where the souls of the cruel, evil or damned go to be tormented and punished for eternity.

Hag Stone – A Hag Stone is a stone that has a naturally formed hole which goes all the way through the stone. In Folklore it is believed that Hag Stones are good luck charms and can protect the carrier from baneful magic and negativity. This comes from the belief that only good things can pass through the hole, because the negative gets stuck in the hole.

Halloween – Halloween is a holiday known as All Hallow's Eve, the day before All Saints Day. Halloween is believed to have its origins in the Celtic celebration of Samhain, a time when the veil before the Living and dead is at its thinnest – 31st October. Halloween has become a very popular holiday for children (young and old) to dress up and get treats. The tradition of dressing up comes from the belief that when you dress up and wear scary masks the demons and evil spirits that walk the earth that night will pass you by, thinking you are one of them.

Hamsa Hand – The Hamsa Hand is an amulet that symbolises the "hand of god" and has its origin in the ancient middle east. The symbol has crossed faiths as a symbol of protection and brings the wearer luck, happiness and general good fortune, all while protecting you from the Evil Eye.

Handfasting – The Handfasting ritual comes from Medieval and Celtic customs in which two people came together to declare their love and intention to marry of their own free will. A Handfasting itself is not legally binding unless the person performing the ritual has become a marriage celebrant or officiant to legalise it. Handfasting have become popular among the Pagan and Spiritual communities.

Hand Parting – If the Handfasting is legally binding, then the couple would have to go through the legal side of separating, however, if the Handfasting wasn't legal and just a celebration of love, then the couple would simply have to declare their intent to separate and have a High Priest or Priestess and community acknowledge the separation.

Harvest Festival – Harvest Festivals are a time to celebrate the abundance and success of crops that year. In the Pagan world we have three harvest festivals beginning in August with Lughnasadh (Lammas) through to Samhain.

- Lughnasadh is the first harvest festival and is associated with grains and grapes.
- Mabon is the second harvest festival, and the one where the majority of yields are collected. Fruits and vegetables, like squashes, apples and (sweet)corn are common.
- Samhain is the final harvest festival and coincides with hunting season, where animals are hunted and their meat prepared for the winter.

Harvest Moon – Traditionally the Harvest Moon is a time when Moonrise comes close to Sunset, which allows a little more time of light in the darkening evenings. The Harvest Moon also refers to the Full Moon that falls closest to the Autumn Equinox.

H

Hearth – The literal meaning of Hearth is the floor of a fireplace, but it is also a place where you call home. It is a place where you are protected, nurtured and nourished on every level – physical, emotional, mental and spiritual.

Hearth Witch – A Hearth Witch is someone who combines the characteristics of Green Witchcraft, Hedge Witchcraft and Kitchen Witchcraft. The Hearth Witch focuses their magic on the home, and welcomes nature into their lives and their dwelling.

Heathen – Heathen is a term that has a number of meanings, and can be used as something derogatory. Heathen can refer to someone who isn't religious, or as someone who doesn't belong to a widely held religion – used especially if someone isn't Christian, Jewish or Muslim. However; Over the last 50-60 years, Pagans have been claiming the word Heathen for those who believe in Germanic and Nordic Paganism or Neo-Paganism.

Hedgewitch – The term Hedgewitch is believed to come from the Saxon word for 'hedge-rider'. While we today refer to a hedge as a boundary of shrubs and plant life, this use of hedge refers to the boundary of the material and spiritual world. A Hedgewitch has a deep knowledge and understanding of the natural world, but they also have a deep knowledge of the Spirit World, or Other World. They walk the boundary between these two realms.

Hellenism – Hellenism refers to the practices and beliefs of those who honour the Greek Gods and Goddesses. During the 20th Century there was a revival of sorts in the beliefs of the ancient Greek people, but like with many modern pagan religious movements, it has been blended with other religious and spiritual practices. It is important to remember that Greeks

Hellenism goes far beyond describing a faith, it is part of their heritage, culture and who they are as a people.

Hereditary Witch – A Hereditary Witch is someone who is part of a family where witchcraft has been passed from one generation to another. You aren't born a witch, and there is no DNA that can indicate that you are, but some families have practices that have been passed from generation to generation. There is a popular theme in the community with people saying;

1. "I descend from the Salem Witches" and unless you have the genetic and historic proof, many won't believe it.
2. "I was born a witch (or Wiccan)" and you may have been born into a family that practices witchcraft, or belong to a Wiccan coven, both require knowledge, experience and learning to join a Wiccan Coven, or to practice alongside family.

Hermetic Order of the Golden Dawn – The Hermetic Order of the Golden Dawn was a secret society in the 19th and early 20th Centuries, who dedicated themselves to the study and practice of the occult, metaphysics and a vague sprinkling of spirituality. One of the most famous members was Aleister Crowley who joined the organisation in 1898. None of the original temples exist anymore, organisations have been established which have carried on and expanded on the teachings and practices. In 1977 Chic Cicero founded The Hermetic Order of the Golden Order INC which still exists to this day.

Hermeticism – Hermeticism is a religious and philosophical movement that has its beliefs rooted in the supposed teachings of Hermes Trismegistus – a figure that blended the beliefs of the Greek God Hermes, and the Egyptian God Thoth. The core beliefs of Hermeticism are that the physical form and its life in the material world is hostile to the soul.

Herbs – A herb is a plant with leaves, seeds and flowers that can be used for flavouring food, creating medicines or as ingredients for perfumes. One characteristic of the herb is that it does not have any woody stems and dies back to the ground after it has flowered. In Witchcraft herbs can be used in spells and rituals, and while some will have beneficial properties, there are some which have not-so-beneficial properties, and these tend to be used in baneful magics.

Herbalism – Herbalism is the study and practice of making medicines and therapies from plants and herbs. The core practice of Herbalism is to use herbs for healing. There are many plants and herbs that are toxic and poisonous, so it is important to know and understand what you are doing.

Herb Bundle – An Herb bundle is a collection of herbs which have been gathered for specific purposes. Herbal bundles can be dried for making incense or in smoke cleansing.

Hex – A Hex is a type of baneful magic, and is focusing on causing unpleasantness (or harm) for the targeted person.

Hexagram – A Hexagram is a six-pointed star, which is formed by two intersecting equilateral triangles, which is also known as The Star of David, and is an important symbol in Judaism. Another form of Hexagram is called a Unicursal Hexagram, which can be drawn in one continuous line, and not by overlaying triangles. Both forms of the Hexagram represent the planetary forces of the macrocosm.

Hexenspiegel – A Hexenspiegel is a small mirror that is used as a protective charm which can reflect any negative energies, the evil eye, and spells back to the sender. Usually, these tiny mirrors are hung on string which can be decorated with crystals, beads and whatever decorative things you want to add. They can be hung on the wall, or they can be carried if they are small enough. The Hexenspiegel is a German Folk custom and is translated to "Witch's Mirror."

High Priest – A High Priest is a male leader or teacher in a community or a coven. They lead rituals, festivals and ceremonies.

High Priestess – A High Priestess is a female leader or teacher of a community. They lead rituals, festivals and ceremonies.

History of Witchcraft – You can describe the history of witchcraft in two different senses;

1. The real-world history of magic and witchcraft, and the witch-craze that spread across Europe in the Middle Ages and Medieval periods. It was illegal to practice witchcraft (The Witchcraft Act 1736) up until 1951 in the UK, which was replaced by the Fraudulent Mediums Act, which was repealed in 2008.
2. The history of magic and magical practices that have been passed down through family bloodlines and communities, these focused on healing and combating baneful magics.

Holding Space – The practice of Holding Space for another person is to be present, open and protective of what another person needs in the moment. It also the process of witnessing and validating someone else's emotional state, while remaining present and aware of your own. When you are holding space for someone, you are doing more than just listening to their woes, or trying to fix them, or giving advice which they haven't asked for. It is actually far more complex. While you are listening to them and offering support, you must remain aware of what you are going through; it's not about taking on their emotions or burdens, and forgetting who you are as an individual.

Homunculus – A Homunculus is a small humanoid creature which has been formed through Alchemy. The first mention of a Homunculus was in the *De Natura Rerum* by Paracelsus in 1537, which outlined the methods of making them. In modern media, you can find them in books, movies and in anime.

Hoodoo – Hoodoo is a form of African American folk magic that is mainly practiced in the Southeastern USA. It focuses on ancestor veneration, saint workshop, herbal medicine and the charming of objects. Hoodoo blends various African spiritualities and indigenous magics and knowledge with influences from Islam, Vodun, and Yoruba.

Horned God – The Horned God is the male counterpart to the Triple Goddess. The Horned God can be seen as an amalgam of Cernunnos, Pan, Inuus and Faunus. These are gods associated with virility, nature, the wilderness, sexuality and hunting.

Horoscope – The Horoscope is a diagram of the planets and signs of the Zodiac any a given time, this is usually associated with the time of your birth. These celestial locations are believed to have an influence on who are, your personality and has been used in fortune telling. The fortunes are usually a broad look at the influences at the time of writing them; and are usually featured in written media like magazines and newspapers.

Hypnosis – Hypnosis is the practice of inducing a state of consciousness where you apparently lose the power to control your body, and is susceptible to suggestion and control – this is more of a stage magic explanation, but hypnosis has been used by psychological professionals to induce a sleep-like state where thoughts flow easier and with professional guidance can be beneficial in mental health fields.

I

Imbolc – Imbolc is the mid-way point between the Winter Solstice and the Vernal Equinox. This is a time when you see the first stirrings of new life, and sense that Spring is coming. Imbolc is one of the Fire Festivals, and is closely associated with the Celtic Goddess Brighid/Brigid, and is celebrated from sundown on the 1st February to sundown on the 2nd February.

Incantation – An incantation is a series of words which are part of a spell or charm, which will trigger a certain effect. The words can be spoken, sung or chanted, whichever you find easier. An incantation can rhyme, but there is no rule that says it has to rhyme. If you choose to sing the incantation, you may find that rhyming can add to the musicality of the incantation.

Incense – Incense is a substance that is burned for the purification and cleansing of a space; it can also be burned for the scent or to aid in meditation. There are a number of forms that incense takes:

- Resin/Gums – These include Frankincense, Copal, Dragon's Blood and Myrrh which are all collected from living trees using tapping, in which a 'tap' is inserted into the trunk during the peak sap season.
- Spices – These come from a range of sources like Cinnamon, Cardamon, Cloves and Fennel are all examples of a Spice incense.
- Herbs – These are plants and flowers gathered and dried for the purpose of burning them.

Other types include nuts, fruits and berries, woods and bark, but these aren't as popular as the above.

When it comes burning incense we have two options, Indirect Burning and Direct Burning:

- Indirect Burning is when you place the raw incense materials which aren't combustible on a charcoal disk, which heats the materials to produce the incense smoke and scent.
- Direct Burning is when the incense materials are burned by a flame, which when extinguished leaves embers which will continue to smoulder, consuming the incense. Direct Burning incense has the widest range of forms, as it can come in cones, sticks, coils and powder.

Incubus – An Incubus is a demonic spirit that is believed to have physical relations with sleeping women. This is the male version of a Succubus.

Initiate – An Initiate is someone who is being inducted into a group, coven or community. To join established Wiccan covens, you often have to go through a process or multiple tests to prove you are ready to join.

Initiation – This is the ritual or ceremony that someone takes on joining and being accepted to a group, community or coven.

Intuition – Intuition is described as knowing something without there being any reason for you to consciously know it, it is something you know instinctively

Invocation – Invocation is often confused with evocation. The difference is when you invoke a spiritual force (like a deity) you are inviting them into your own body, while when you evoke a spiritual force, you are only welcoming them into your circle or ritual space.

J

Jar Spells – A jar spell is exactly what it sounds like, a spell that has been enclosed in a jar. These can be placed in a specific place – like the freezer, or carried as a good luck or protection charm. Jar spells can contain a range of things from crystals, herbs, salts and other items. When making a spell jar, you need to think about what ingredients you want to use. *For me there are two main types of jar spell, a "wet" jar, and a "dry" jar.*

- A wet jar contains mostly liquids which have been blended for specific reasons. A freezer spell is a type of wet jar, as you are using water.
- A dry jar contains mostly dry ingredients like herbs, crystals and salts. A self-love spell will contain crystals, herbs and colours which all support self-love.

Jamais Vu – Jamais Vu is the opposite of déjà vu, it is the experience of feeling something is unfamiliar, even though it is very familiar to you.

Jinx – A jinx is a form of baneful magic which causes the target to suffer bad luck. It is also used to describe someone who has particularly bad luck, which causes trouble for others.

Juju – In common usage, juju refers to good or bad luck which stem from a person's deed, spell or charm. It is also used to describe someone's vibe and aura. If we move away from common usage and look towards the roots of the word, a Juju is a charm or fetish which is believed to have magical powers by West African people.

Jinn/Djinn – A Jinn is an intelligent magical spirit, which may appear in human form or as an animal. These spirits are believed to be able to possess a person, and are feared in Arabian and Muslim culture. The Jinn can be summoned and invoked for a multitude of reasons, but many in Arabic countries fear them. The Genie is an Anglicised name of Jinn/Djinn and while the spirits have the same core, a Genie has now become synonymous with a being which grants three wishes. Genies can be tricksters, and grant the wishes, not always how the person expected, so it is important in these stories for the one wishing to be very clear and precise with their wishes.

K

Karma – In Hindu and Buddhist beliefs, Karma is the sum of a person's actions, in this and all previous incarnations; and how these actions are viewed as deciding one's fate after death. It is also used to denote the good or bad luck someone has as a result of their actions.

Kemetism – Kemetism is a neo-pagan religion which is based on the religion of Ancient Egypt which appeared in the mid to late 20th Century. There are five core tenants to Kemetism, which are; Upholding the laws of Ma'at, the belief in Netjer (a supreme being which all Ancient Egyptian gods and goddesses are part of), the veneration of Akhu/ancestors and the participation in and respect for the community.

Kettle – A Kettle is a smaller vessel similar to a cauldron which is hung over a fire by an arc shaped handle. Today, kettles tend to be used for boiling water, which can be used to make a variety of things, and is an important tool for a kitchen witch.

Key – A key is a small piece of metal which has indentations carved into it which can be used to open or close a lock. As a mechanism for open and closing something, a key can be used to represent liberation, knowledge, mystery, power, insight. They can also be used to 'unlock' barriers and blocks which may be hindering you.

Kitchen Witch – A Kitchen Witch is someone whose magic is focused and mainly practiced in the kitchen. They weave magic into all of their creations, whether it is an intricately planned spell, a simple cup of tea or in the meals they make.

Knife – A knife is a sharpened blade which represents power, strength, honour and nobility. While many witches have an athame for ritual work, the cutting of herbs, for example, is done by a knife

Knot Magic – Knot Magic has a simple premise; you create knots in a cord to create representations of your intent in spells and rituals. While creating knots is important, so is the chord you choose and the colour of the cord. The placement, number and pattern of the knots will all have meanings to the practitioner, and they all help to empower the magic. Some choose to recite incantations after tying the knot to further empower the magic. As long as the knots remains unbroken or undone, the magic and energies called are active, but as soon as the cord or knots deteriorate, the magic becomes weaker and/or broken. Knot magic is believed to be one of the simplest and oldest forms of magic, but while it is simple it is hard to pin down when it was first recorded, let alone used.

L

Lady – This is an honorific title given to the Goddess in Wicca. For some covens, the female leader may be given the title of lady for her dedication to the coven and community.

Lammas – Lammas is another name for the Celtic festival of Lughnasadh. It's also known as Loaf Mass in Christian circles.

Lampadomancy – Lampadomancy is a form of divination which focuses on the flame and the soot and carbon deposits left by a burning lamp or candle. It was very popular in Ancient Egypt.

Left Hand Path – The Left Hand Path is described as rejecting the conventions of society, and embrace techniques and magical practices which are seen as or considered taboo by wider society. Sex magic, and using it in a magical and ritual sense, is one example of embracing something that is seen as taboo by wider society. The use of Satanic imagery can also be considered as going against the societal norm.

Lenormand – Lenormand is a form of divination called Cartomancy, and while it is similar to tarot and oracle cards, they also differ significantly. While tarot focuses on the broader aspects of life, Lenormand focuses primarily on the day-to-day happenings, and the practical aspects of life. When reading Lenormand, the relationship between cards and their relationships are extremely important.

Lesser Sabbat – The Lesser Sabbats are the Solar celebrations in the Wheel of the Year, which means the Solstices and Equinoxes. Just because lesser is part of the name, this doesn't mean they are any less important in the wheel.

Lesser Key of Solomon – *The Lesser Key of Solomon* is a magical grimoire which is attributed to King Solomon, but likely dates back to the Middle Ages to early Medieval period. The book is split into two parts. *Book One* contains the conjurations and invocations to summon and constrain demons and the spirits of the departed. The entities that are summoned are compelled to do whatever the summoner wishes, from finding something that has been lost to gaining power. *Book Two* is focused on what the summoner/caster needs to do before they are able to do any of the summoning, from purifying the body and what clothes are needed to be worn to what you need to do with the tools gathered.

Ley Lines – A Ley Line (also called Mana Line) is a straight line which connects three or more prehistoric or ancient spiritual sites. These lines that connect spiritual sites are associated with high amounts of energy and a plethora of paranormal and supernatural events, and can cause people to have unexplainable experiences.

Litha – Litha is the festival which celebrates the start of summer and the Summer Solstice. The date of the solstice varies due to the Sun and the time where it reaches the peak of daylight hours. The celebrations seem to have been borrowed from a range of cultures, but most cultures celebrated the Summer Solstice in some way.

Lithomancy – Lithomancy is a form of divination which uses stones and the light that is reflected from them, and historically has been popular in the UK. The first verified accounts of Lithomancy were a patriarch of Constantinople, but others claim that Helen of Troy predicted the fall and destruction of Troy using Lithomancy.

Lord – This is an honorific title given to the God in Wicca. For some covens, the male leader may be given the title of lord for his dedication to the coven and community. Lord is also used as a title for the Christian God too.

Love Spell – Love spells are designed to attract love, but there is always an ethical conversation that needs to be had when casting love spells. If you are casting a spell on someone without their knowledge or consent, you can take their free will, and the right to make their own choices. If you are casting a love spell on yourself to promote self-love, then the water is far less murky as you are casting it with the full understanding and knowledge of the outcome.

Lucid Dreaming – Lucid dreaming happens when a dreamer realises, they are, in fact, dreaming, which allows them to have a modicum of control over the dream and what is happening.

Lughnasadh – Lughnasadh is the first of the harvest festivals, and falls around the 1st August in the Northern Hemisphere. This is a time when the first harvests are collected and stored, and it is closely associated with grains and grapes. The Celtic festival of Lughnasadh is associated with the god Lugh, who is the god of the sun and light.

Lunar Eclipses – A Lunar Eclipse occurs when the Moon moves into the Earth's shadow, which means that the Earth is between the Sun and Moon, which causes a show to appear over the moon.

- Partial Lunar Eclipse – A Partial Lunar Eclipse occurs when the Moon passes through the darkest part of the Moon's shadow, especially the cone shaped region of full shadow. A Partial Lunar Eclipse is easily seen by the naked eye as the Moon may have a reddish hue.

- Penumbral Lunar Eclipse – A Penumbral Lunar Eclipse occurs when the Moon passes through the faint outer part of the Earth's shadow, and this means that only part of the Sun's rays is obscured.
- Total Lunar Eclipse – A Total Lunar Eclipse occurs when the whole Moon passes into the Earth's shadow and the rays of the Sun are fully obscured, which caused the whole moon to have a reddish hue. It's because of this hue that some refer to a Total Lunar Eclipse as a Blood Moon.

Lupercalia – Lupercalia is a festival that was celebrated on the 15th February in Ancient Rome, and while it does fall around the same time as Valentines Day, Lupercalia is far from lovey-dovey. It is a bloody, violent and sexually charged affair, brimming with animal sacrifice, and people coupling up to ward off evil spirits and infertility by picking names from a bowl. It is widely thought that the origin comes from the Latin for Wolf, which is Lupus. it is also suggested that there could be a connection to the she-wolf who raised the creators of Rome, Romulus and Remus.

M

Mabon – Mabon is the second of the harvest festivals of the Wheel of the Year, and falls on the Autumnal Equinox. The time and date of the Equinox changes from year to year because it depends on when the Sun crosses the Celestial Equator.

Magi – A Magi is a member of a religious or priestly caste from Persia. The "Three Kings" from the Nativity story are believed to have been Magi from Persia. It is also another name for a sorcerer.

Magick – In the early 20th Century Aleister Crowley used to spell magic with a K at the end to denote its difference to stage magic. Today many witches, pagans and magic(k) practitioners use a K at the end to differentiate it from the fictional sort of magic that is prevalent in popular culture.

Maiden – The Maiden is an aspect of the Triple Goddess, and she is depicted as a young, innocent, full of enthusiasm and hopeful figure, who is closely associated with the Dawn, Spring and virginity.

Maleficium – The literal definition of Maleficium is "evil doing", so in the world of witchcraft it would be someone who practices malevolent, dangerous and harmful magic. Basically, if someone practices Baneful Magic, they can be referred to as a Maleficium.

Malleus Maleficarum – This is a book written in the late 15th Century by Heinrich Kramer, and is known as *The Hammer of Witches,* and was essentially a witch hunting manual and instructions on how to find, catch, interrogate and "deal" with witches. While there are other earlier publications on how to find witches, the *Malleus Maleficarum* was so widespread because of the invention of the printing press by Johannes Gutenberg.

Mantra – The term Mantra literally means "sacred utterance" and is a word or sound that is used to help you in meditation, especially if you find concentration hard. The more you use a Mantra, the more it with stick with you.

May Pole – A May Pole is a tall and often painted (though that isn't necessary) pole which is decorated with flowers and long ribbons attached to the top, which when held during the dance create an intricate pattern around it. The May Pole represents the God, as it is phallic symbol, while the ribbons represent the Goddess. The May Pole Dance encourages fertility and brings a community together.

Meditation – Meditation is the practice of clearing your mind using a range of techniques, and these techniques can be breathing, guided meditation or physical movement like dance. The practice itself is thousands of years old and is an aspect of a number of world religions, even Christianity has its own name for it, Contemplation. You can find guided meditations online which can help you begin your meditation journey.

Medium – In the world of Spirituality a person who is believed to be able to contact with Spirits is called a Medium. They are the ones who guide séances, or act as an intermediary between the living and the world of spirits. They may be able to see, hear or experience the emotions of a spirit which is then conveyed to the living.

Megalith – A Megalith is a stone that has been used to build an ancient or prehistoric structure – they are the building blocks for many spiritual sites across the world. Stonehenge (around 5,000 years old) in England and Göbekli Tepe (around 11,500 years old) in Turkey are both examples of Megalithic Structures.

Meridian – There are a number of meanings for Meridian. 1) A Meridian is a circular line that passes through the North and South poles. The Prime Meridian is a line that runs from the North pole to the South pole, and passes through Greenwich in the UK. This is known as Greenwich Mean Time, or GMT. 2) In a variety of Chinese medicine practices, a Meridian is a channel which is part of a network in the body though which Chi/Ki/Qi flows.

Merry Meet – This is a greeting that many Witches use when greeting other witches, essentially it is like saying hello to someone else within the community, as long as it is not something unpleasant – like a funeral. It can also be used when closing a circle as "Merry Meet, Merry part and Merry Meet Again". It is believed that this saying came from an article written by Lady Gwen Porter in a poem called "The Rede of the Wiccae" in which it states "Merry Meet and Merry Part, Bright the Cheeks, and Warm the Heart." The Rede of the Wiccae, published in issue 69 of the Green Egg Magazine in 1975

Meso-Paganism – This is a group which has been inspired and influenced by a number of world views and belief systems. Monotheism, Dualism, and Nontheistic beliefs. Indigenous Peoples belief systems fit into this category, as does New Age spirituality, and in a broad sense, even Traditional Wicca can fit.

Metaphysical – If something is to be classed as Metaphysical, it means it can't be classified by objective and repetitive study of material realities. Things like the study of space and time, the study of existence and reality are examples of what falls under the term Metaphysical studies.

Mid-Summer – Mid-Summer is another term for the Summer Solstice, and is different from the Mid-point of Summer which falls between 1st and 6th of August. *If you are in the Southern Hemisphere, Mid-Summer falls between the* 1st *and* 6th *February.*

Mid-Winter – Mid Winter is another term for the Winter Solstice, and is different from the mid-point of Winter, which falls between the 1st and 6th of February. *If you live in the Southern Hemisphere, Mid-Winter falls between the* 1st *and* 6th *August.*

Mineral – A mineral is a naturally occurring substance that is not organic in nature. Quartz, Calcite, Fluorite, and Hematite are all examples of minerals, but not all of them are crystals.

Mjolnir – Mjolnir, also known as Thor's Hammer. Thor's Hammer has become so well-known and popular in the modern mainstream thanks to the Marvel franchise that features Thor and his magical hammer, for which Thor had to shed his Ego to be worthy of wielding it. In mythology, the weapon is made by two dwarves' brothers and while the forging process was happening, Loki did his best to sabotage its creation by biting the eyelid of one of the dwarven Smith's eyes. It's due to this that Mjolnir has a shorter handle and is wielded in one hand. Even with this Mjolnir is considered the most powerful weapon in the Universe.

Mojo – The Mojo often used in everyday language means having a special quality that makes them really good at something. However, in the world of magic and witchcraft a Mojo is a spell, charm or talisman from which a person can benefit from.

Mojo Bag – An aspect of Hoodoo and other African-American spiritual practices, a Mojo bag is a magical charm bag that can be used for many reasons, from protection, to healing, to cause harm and to manifest something. What is placed inside the bag, will depend on what you are creating the bag for.

Moon – The Moon is a natural satellite of a planet, which is primarily visible at night thanks to it reflecting the light of the Sun. In our solar system there are more than 470 satellites like the Moon.

Moon Phases – The Moon is ever changing in the night sky because of its orbit around the Earth, and's shape and size in the night sky has its own meaning.

- The New Moon – The New Moon is the time to set your intentions for the upcoming lunar cycle.
- The Waxing Crescent Moon – The Crescent Moon is the time when your resolve deepens regarding your intentions.
- The First Quarter – The First Quarter is the time to put plans into action and start moving toward your goal.
- The Waxing Gibbous Moon – The Gibbous is a time to refine and improve on the processes that you have in place.
- The Full Moon – The Full Moon is a time when you take stock and let realizations come to you about the success (or failure) of your goals.
- Disseminating Moon (The Waning Gibbous Moon) – The Disseminating Moon is a time where you can express new found truths and how you can learn from them, and let go of what's not working
- The Last Quarter – The Last Quarter of the Moon is the time to prepare for the next cycle of the Moon by preparing the seeds of for future plans and goals

- Balsamic Moon (The Waning Crescent Moon) – The Balsamic Moon is the time where you prepare and ready yourself in quiet and stillness before the Moon begins its new cycle

Monotheism – Monotheism is the belief in one God. Christianity, Judaism, and Islam are all monotheistic religions, all with a common deity. One of the first recorded monotheistic religions was in Ancient Egypt, where Akanaten changed the national religion to worship the Aten, and the Aten alone.

Mother – The Mother is an aspect of the Triple Goddess, and as the mother she is associated with maturity, nurturing, fertility and productivity. She is associated with the fullness of the earth and the harvest season.

Muggle – This is a relatively new word to the world of witchcraft thanks to *Harry Potter*, it is now in common use when witches describe someone who isn't familiar with the craft.

Mundane – The literal meaning of mundane, is to explain how something is not very interesting, dull or not exciting. In general use among witches, calling someone or something mundane, means you are saying they lack something magical. While it is part of a popular literature, it has been part of the English language since the Middle Ages, and it's meaning has not strayed.

Mutable Sign – Mutable Signs refer to Gemini. Virgo, Sagittarius and Pisces. Mutable Signs are able to adapt to evolving situations and excel at navigating change. The Mutable Signs fall before the changing of the seasons, and see the positive things to come, rather than focusing on the actual changes.

Mystic – A Mystic is someone who is seeking a direct experience with the Sacred, without anyone mediating, or acting as an intermediary or catalyst.

Mysticism – Mysticism is the experience of communing or union with a higher power – whatever that power may be. This communion, or union can be facilitated through chanting, contemplation, prayer or meditation.

Myth – A myth is a traditional story that focuses on gods, goddesses, heroes or figures that represent aspects of everyday life. Myths tend to be unfounded stories that reflect the beliefs of the culture they are from. In Greek Mythology after boasting she was better at weaving than Athena, the goddess challenged Arachne to a weaving context, and because Arachne's weaving was outstanding, Athena turned her into a Spider because of her hubris and for what she depicted in her weaving. None of the gods wanted their dirty deeds and dealings laid bare for the world to see. *This is a story that explains why spiders weave intricate webs.*

Mythology – Mythology is a collection of myths which belong to a region, culture or religion. The Ancient Greeks has a very different set of myths to the Celts and Ancient Britons, because their lives were different, and the stories often depicted the landscape as part of the mythology.

N

Necromancy – Necromancy is the belief and practice of communicating and controlling the dead, usually for foretelling purposes. In fiction, Necromancy is the practice of raising the dead for nefarious purposes, mainly as a weapon.

Necronomicon – While not directly associated with Witchcraft, but a very popular fiction writer HP Lovecraft. It is commonly believed to mean *Book of Dead Names,* and it is believed to summon monsters and horrific deities.

Neo-Paganism – Neo-Paganism is a modern religious movement which focuses on the beliefs, practices and rituals from older religions which sit outside of the Abrahamic religions. Some Neo-Pagans like to stick to one culture in their beliefs, while others like to draw from more than one.

New Age – New Age is a range of beliefs and practices that seemed to develop during and after the 1970's, and is characterised by the eclectic nature of their beliefs one thing that is always present is the emphasis of the "authority of self" and taking responsibility for the impact you have on the world. The New Age movement commonly believe that non-human beings like Angels, can communicate with us.

Nine Herb Charm – The Nine Herb Charm is a spell which was used to promote healing and ward off diseases. The herbs used in in this charm are: Camomile, Nettle, Fennel, Crab Apple, Mugwort, Plantain, Watercress and Chervil. The God Odin/Woden was called upon in the spell to give the herbs power.

Nocturnal Magic – Nocturnal Magic is also known as night magic, as it is usually practiced after the sun goes down and the Moon rises. People that practice Nocturnal Magic have said that there is something different from practicing in the day. They may not be able to put their finger on why, but the night is quiet, which allows a different kind of connection, from the noise of the daytime.

Numerology – Numerology is the study of numbers, and the belief that each number has its own individual meaning, but the combination of numbers has meaning too. A popular form of numerology is finding your Life Path Number, which is calculated from the numbers of your date of birth. Example: *My date of birth is 20th February 1987, so that will look like this; 2+0+0+2+1+9+8+7 = and that equals 29, which we add those numbers together 2+9 = 11 and you can add those together too 1+1 = 2. According to this, my Life Path Number is either 11 or 2 depending on how far you wish to go.*

O

Oath – An Oath is a promise made, a solemn vow made with sincerity and honesty. For a witch, an oath is a binding promise, and is by its nature sacred, as they form a bond which may be overseen by a divine force.

Occult – The Occult is a very broad umbrella which covers a number of different avenues of study which include (but not limited to) Esoterica, the Supernatural, Magic(k) and Mysticism. Some would characterise Witchcraft and Astrology as realms of the Occult.

Offering – The literal meaning of offering is "a thing offered to something greater than the self". When you give something as an offering, you are doing so freely as a show of love, devotion or respect. You do not make an offering in order to get something in return, it is not transactional in nature. When you leave an offering to a tree you took branches from, it is a thank you for those branches, it shows your gratitude and reverence for the tree and its growth.

Old Wives Tale – An Old Wives tale is a story that has been handed down the generations which often relate to superstitions of the region. Example: *using a pendulum to "divine" what the sex of a neighbour's baby would be. She was convinced it was a boy, but I told her from the way the pendulum was swinging it was a girl, and I was right. She now has a beautiful daughter.*

Olympian Gods – The Olympian Gods were the third generation of gods in Ancient Greece. They were all the children of Rhea and Cronos; the latter ate each of the children soon after birth to avoid a prophecy. Zeus was saved from that fate by

Rhea, and as a grown god, he came to rescue his siblings. He became King of the Gods of Olympus. Hades, Hestia, Demeter, Poseidon, and Hera were all freed from his belly by Zeus. These six figures became the predominant gods and goddesses along with Aphrodite, Athena, Artemis, Apollo, Ares, Hephestus and Dionysus, but these were not a product of Rhea and Cronos' coupling.

Omen – An omen is a message which is regarded as a portent of something good, or bad. There are times when omens are seen to have prophetic qualities. According to superstition, omens can predict good things as often as they do bad things. An example of an omen is the belief that if a black cat crosses your path, means bad luck is soon to follow.

Omnism – This is the belief in all gods of every religion. So, someone who follow this path believes in, for example, all the Greek, Roman, Norse and Egyptian deities.

Oneiromancy – Oneiromancy is a form of divination which uses dreams to foretell the future. One of the most famous examples of Oneiromancy is actually the story of Joseph and his Technicolour Dreamcoat. Pharah asks him to explain what his dream means, and thanks to Joseph, the land of Egypt is spared the wrath of famine.

Oomancy – Oomancy is a form of divination which uses eggs to foretell the future. A separated egg is dropped into a pan of hot water and the shapes and forms it takes have meanings. I have heard that Oomancy can be used to see if someone has fallen under the Evil Eye.

Oracle – An oracle is a medium through which advice, counsel and/or prophecy is given. The most popular oracle in mythology and historically would be the Oracle (Pythia) of Delphi, who were the "mouthpiece" of Apollo.

Oracle Cards – Oracle decks are very different from Tarot, they have no set structure, they have no set number of cards. they are created pretty much from scratch by the author/artist. Most, if not all Oracle decks have a theme, whether it be healing, guidance, messages. They have a wide range of artistic themes as well, from the Fae to dragons, crystals to animal guides. They tend to look at the bigger picture, while other forms like tarot and Lenormand look at different aspects in the bigger picture.

Ostara – Ostara is another name for the Spring Equinox and fall on or around the 21st March. The time and date of the Equinox changes from year to year because it depends on when the Sun crosses the Celestial Equator. Ostara focuses on the new life of Spring, new beginnings, renewal, rebirth and fertility.

Other World – The Other World is a place that is beyond reality or a world beyond death. Valhalla and Sessrúmnir are the halls of Odin and Freyja respectively in Norse Mythology. Tír na nÓg (Irish) and Annwn (Welsh) are both names of Celtic other worlds.

Ouija Board – A Ouija Board is a board with letters and numbers across the middle of the board and someone will be the words Yes and No. A planchette or a pointer of some kind is used to indicate the letters in a séance. The people around the table all place a single finger on the pointer to give the "spirits" energy to move it.

Ouroboros – The Ouroboros is depicted as a snake or dragon which is consuming its own tail. It is a symbol that represents the eternal cycle of birth, growth, death for the cycle to begin again. Sometimes the Ouroboros is depicted as a circle, or as a figure eight or the infinity symbol.

Out of Body Experience – The literal definition of "Out of Body" experience, if the sensation of being outside of one's body. It could be a floaty feeling, or like you are seeing yourself from a distance. There have been many reports of people who are near death, or experience something that brings them to that brink say they've had experiences. Astral Projection can also be considered a form of Outer Body Experience, because you are actively leaving your physical or conscious form.

P

Pagan – When it comes to the definition of what "pagan" means, it gets a little complicated because it has had a number of meanings throughput history.

- In Antiquity the term pagan was believed to be used to describe someone who didn't practice Christianity. This could be because they practiced polytheism in more rural areas, where Christianity hadn't reached, or followed an ethnic or regional practice.
- In the Middle Ages, the term was used to refer to anyone who didn't follow a Christian religion (some sources say Abrahamic religion, which include Judaism and Islam).
- During the 19th Century there was resurgence of Greco-Roman art and those who were inspired by this style sometimes referred to themselves as Pagan.
- In the last 120 years, there has been a revival of beliefs and practices from the ancient world. Many of the modern Pagan beliefs lie in nature worship alongside the views of Pantheism, Panentheism, Polytheism, Animism, while some do follow some form of monotheism.

Paganism – Paganism refers to the path that a Pagan follows, but today it is more of an umbrella term from which many different paths like Wicca fall under.

Palo Santo – Palo Santo refers to wood from the Bursera Graveolens tree, and was named Palo Santo by the months that found it, which means "Holy Wood", "Holy Stick" or "Wood of the Saints". It has been used in rituals for centuries for cleansing bad energies, and to ward of negativity. In recent years it has been classified as in critical danger due to over harvesting. The government of Peru permits the collection of naturally fallen or dead trees. Efforts are being made to plant and protect new trees, but illegal collection of the tree is happening due to the demand for its cleansing properties. *The use of Palo Santo has been considered a closed practice for a while now, and I am not an expert on its production, collection or cultural significance. I have been gifted some chips of Palo Santo, which I know was harvested ethically has the person collected it themselves while in Peru.*

Palmistry – Palmistry (often called Palm Reading) is the art of reading the lines and features on the palm of the hand. It is believed that how the lines intersect can tell you a lot about who you are and what your future may hold.

Pantheism – Pantheism actually has two main definitions. 1) is the belief that everything in the Universe (including nature) is the same as a Divinity, or a Supreme God/dess, or at least a manifestation of God. 2) is the belief in all gods of every religion, but this is often better known as Omnism.

Panentheism – Panentheism is the belief that the Divine touches, connects and traverses every part of the universe and transcends that we know as space and time.
Note *While Pantheism says that God is equal to the universe, and is part of God, Panentheism says that God is greater than the Universe, a truly supreme being.*

Pantheon – A Pantheon refers to the divinities of a region or culture. Pantheons are usually Polytheistic in nature, as it's the worship and veneration of many gods and goddesses.

Paranormal – Paranormal refers to something that can't be explained using science. The Paranormal (like Paganism) is an umbrella term, for which many terms sit under. ESP, telepathy, spiritualism, ghost and cryptid hunting and even UFO's. There is a wealth of media about searching for the paranormal, and like many things in our world, you need to make your own mind up about the paranormal and what you believe does and doesn't exist

Path – The term path has a number of meanings, and I think they all boil down to a path being a route laid out that someone walks along. This can be a literal path from place A to B or it can be more metaphorical. In a metaphorical sense it is the type of witchcraft you practice, or the magical work you do. Example, *I have chosen to walk the path of a Rainbow Witch – while some may say it's the same as a Grey Witch, I think it differs because, I don't choose the middle route, walking the line of black and white. I celebrate the whole spectrum, seen and unseen.*

Patron God/Goddess – Over the centuries the meaning of a Patron God or Goddess has changed. In antiquity a Patron God is a deity that protects the city, town or village. Every home and hearth were sacred to Hestia, so she guarded and protected all homes as well as seats of government. Athena was the Patron Goddess of Athens. Helios was the Patron God of Rhodes. In a modern sense, a patron deity is a god or goddess that has taken a particular interest in you and the development of your spirituality, and it has been known that once their role in your development is complete, they may step back for another to come forward. You can have multiple patrons at the same time, as long as they hold a relevance in your life and spiritual practice.

Pendulum – In a literal sense, a pendulum is a weight that is held by a fixed point (usually a string) so it can swing freely. The pendulum has been used since ancient times as a way of keeping the time, generating power, diving the future and as a way of measuring something. A pendulum can be made from a variety of materials including wood, metal and crystals, and can be homemade. The old wives' tale about holding a ring on a string to determine the baby's sex acts like a pendulum. If it swings back and forth, it's a boy. If it swings in a circle, it's a girl.

Pentacle – The Pentacle is possibly the most popular and famous symbols associated with witchcraft. A Pentacle is a five-sided star within a circle, and what it means may differ slightly from witch-to-witch, but in general, the pentacle is a representation of the four natural elements Earth, Air, Fire, Water and the fifth point (the upward facing point) is a representation of Spirit, (or Aether or Akasha). The circle represents bringing all these things together, the unity of them all. *An easy way to remember where the elements are placed is to go alphabetically around the symbol, with Spirit always at the apex, or top point of the star.*

Pentagram – A Pentagram is a five-sided star, and like with the pentacle the five points represent the five elements. The different factor of the pentagram is that it does not have a circle surrounding the star. There are two main types of pentagrams, the Invoking Pentagram and the Banishing Pentagram, and the type you draw depends on where you start. For example, if you are invoking the fire element you start at the top point, and draw towards the bottom left point, which represents fire before continuing the star. If you are banishing the fire element, you start at the point that represents fire and start to draw away from that point before continuing with the star.

Penumbra – The Penumbra is the outer regions of shadow which is cast by a light source, including the Sun. When an eclipse falls in this area it is known as a Penumbral Eclipse.

Pestle & Mortar – A Pestle and Mortar are tools which are used to grind substances into powder or a paste. The Mortar is the bowl, and the Pestle is the club-like implement used to pound the ingredients. In Witchcraft the pestle and mortar can represent the union of the masculine (pestle) and feminine (mortar), and it is a place of transformation and change as the separate ingredients are added to become something new and different.

Perigee – Perigee is a term that is used in Astronomy to refer to the Moon or a satellite being at its closest point to the Earth. When a Full or New Moon occurs when the Moon is in Perigee then we call it a Super Moon because the Moon looks bigger and brighter than normal.

Phantom – The literal meaning of phantom is an apparition, spectre or a ghost. It's not as popular as other terms, but it can still catch you out if you're reading older books on the spiritual world.

Philosopher's Stone – While we are familiar with the Philosopher's Stone thanks to *Harry Potter,* it is something that Alchemists of old tried to create in order to change base metals into gold. Some alchemists believed that it could cure all diseases and prolong life to an extreme degree. The creation of the Philosopher's Stone was seen as the Great Work or Magnum Opus of Alchemy, which means it was the goal of all forms of Alchemy.

Planchette – While the Planchette is known to be the paddle-shaped pointer that accompanies Ouija Boards, but the term refers to a tool used in Automatic Writing. It is still a heart-shaped piece of wood, which is placed on casters for free movement and a hole which will hold a pen or pencil. When

Ouija boards became popular at séances, the media at the time claimed it was the "new planchette", and the creators never intended for it to take the Planchette's place.

Planets 'the' – The Planets are celestial bodies that revolve around a sun, and each has its motions, which is unique to the planet. In Astrology each planet has its own meaning, and can represent dives and urges in our lives. The zodiac sign that is in the different planetary houses at the time of your birth is believed to hold information about the person you are and the varying facets of the conscious and subconscious mind.

Planetary Hours – This is a very old system of Astrology which dictates that each of the classical planets are given a day of the week to rule over, but they are also associated with different times of the day too.

Planetary Houses – The Planetary Houses is as Astrological term that refer to the twelve sections of a birth chart. Each house has an associated ruler, and these both will depend on the time and location of your birth, and when creating an accurate birth chart, these are vital. Otherwise, there is a margin of error which could derail the chart.

Polytheism – Polytheism is the belief in many gods, and in the belief of many gods, a single figure might become more dominant like Zeus of Ancient Greece, who became King of the Gods. Hinduism, Taoism, Shintoism are all modern Polytheistic religions. In the ancient world the religions of the Greeks, Romans, Egyptians, Celts, Aztecs etc... are all examples of polytheistic religions.

Poppet – A Poppet in witchcraft is a small figure or a doll that is to be used in a spell. They can be made from a range of materials from a potato to clay and from a carved root to cloth which has been sewn and stuffed. They are believed to be a bridge between the physical world and the spirit world, and have been used in folk magic and other forms of sympathetic magic for centuries. A poppet can be made for beneficial magic such as healing and attracting abundance, or it can be made for baneful magic such as hexes and curses.

Possession – The literal meaning of possession is the ownership of something regardless of whether or not it is yours. In a spiritual sense it is the belief that a spirit, deity, demon or other spiritual being has entered your body without permission and has garnered control of your body. Changes in behaviour, mental and physical health can be seen by those around you. For some, the only way to remedy a possession is to perform an exorcism.

Potion – A potion is a liquid concoction that is believed to have magical powers, which will have an effect on the drinker. Potions have been part of folklore and mythology for a very long time, however, today they are seen in popular media and stories. You could call an herbal tea blend as a potion, as you are adding ingredients with healing or beneficial properties to water. Oh, tea is a magical potion… I knew it!

Precognition – Precognition is the ability to know something will happen before it occurs, without causing it to happen. There is no scientific proof that people are able to do this, but those who have had experiences, can't explain them either.

Priest – A Priest is an ordained male leader, teacher and officials of a church or gathering. Usually associated with Christianity, but in the world of spirituality, it's usually a High Priest.

Priestess – A Priestess is a female leader, teacher and officials of a non-Christian religion or community.

Primordial Gods – Primordial means something has existed from the beginning of time. So, these are the first generation of gods in a pantheon or religion. These are more abstract concepts than what came after, for example, in Greek mythology Gaia is the primordial goddess of the Earth. She is the personification of the Earth. In Ancient Egypt they believed that the first gods came to Earth in pairs, and it is these pairs that created the world.

Projective Hand – The Projective hand is sometimes known as the dominant hand, and this is usually determined by which hand you write with. This is the hand that energy flows from the body. If you are drawing a circle for a spell or ritual work, you would use an Athame in your dominant hand. It gets complicated if you are ambidextrous, but if you are, take a deep breath and reach for something, whatever hand you instinctively reach with is your dominant hand, and the other is the receptive hand.

Psychic – The term psychic is two-fold. On one hand it refers to something that is relating to the psyche, whether it being mental or spiritual – in Greek Mythology the Psyche was used as the definition of the human soul. The other is when someone claims to have special abilities that go beyond scientific reasoning and experimentation. Mediumship, Clairvoyance, and Telepathy all fall under the Psychic umbrella.

Psychopomp – A psychopomp comes from a Greek term which literally means a "guide of souls". The Psychopomp are figures who guide the souls of the newly transitioned into the afterlife.

The Psychopomp can be found in religions and belief systems from all over the world. These figures can be: Angels, Spirits, Demons, Deities, Anthropomorphic entities and even other humans. Humans have always found the prospect of death both frightening and fascinating, and these figures provide comfort and guidance to those who have passed on. They give the dying person the knowledge that there is a compassionate being that will help them through their transition. They also provide comfort for the living, knowing their loved ones will be taken care of at the end of their life.

Psychic Vampires – A Psychic vampire is someone who drains you of energy, and while people can do this maliciously, by purposefully draining those around them. Some people don't realise they can do it to people and have no control over it.

Purification – When you are purifying something you are removing anything that is impure, or is contaminating the space, person or object. In the Spiritual world, when you are purifying something, you are doing rituals to make something spiritually clean. *Purifying is a deeper more ritualised version of cleansing, but can be deeply interconnected.*

Q

Qabalah – The Qabalah is an ancient Jewish tradition that is based on esoteric interpretation of the Torah (or the Old Testament). Today Hermetic Qabalah/Kabballah is influenced by this ancient Jewish mysticism, western astrology, alchemy and a dozen other traditions and disciplines. Those who do practice are on their own journey to find the "light" within themself.

Quarters – The Quarters refer to calling on the elemental guardians of the cardinal compass directions. They are also known as guardians or watchtowers. The practice of calling the Quarters originated with the Hermetic Order of the Golden Dawn, but has since been adopted by Wiccans, Pagans and Witches of all kinds. Usually, you begin in the East with Air, and move round clockwise (or Deosil) to South and Fire, West and Water and finally North and Earth. To dismiss the Quarters, you do this in reverse, starting with North and moving anti-clockwise (or widdershins). It is very important that you thank each of the Spirits of the Quarters.

Quartz – Quartz is a mineral consisting of Silicon Dioxide. It has a very ordered hexagonal structure which produces the characteristic clusters and points we are used to seeing. Quartz has a hardness of seven on the Moh's Scale, which means it is harder than Feldspar and Orthoclase, but isn't as hard as Corundum (Ruby and Sapphire) and Diamonds. A standard nail made of steel is not hard enough to scratch the surface of a piece of Quartz.

Quicksilver – Quicksilver is another name for the liquid state of Mercury, which is believed to have originated in Alchemy. In Alchemy, Quicksilver was associated with the planet and Roman God Mercury, who was linked to speed and mobility. Mercury is the fastest planet to orbit the Sun.

R

Reading – I would love to make a quip about you are reading about reading, but I shall refrain. I am referring to what you receive from someone who uses tarot, oracle cards, palms, tea leaves... to garner information for you. This is a reading. The person doing the reading is known as a "reader" and they "read" the messages and information that is coming forth for you.

Receptive Hand – The Receptive Hand is the opposite of the Projective Hand, and is the hand that you receive energy through. If you are right-handed, then your Receptive hand is your left hand. If you are left-handed, your receptive hand will be your right hand. As I mentioned with the Projective hand, the dominant hand is what you reach for something with when you are ambidextrous, so the non-dominant hand is the one you don't reach with.

Rede – The literal meaning of Rede is to give counsel, advice or share wisdom with another, but in the world of witches, Rede refers to the Wiccan Rede. Originally the Rede was the eight-word couplet which Doreen Valiente recorded in 1964. *"Eight words the Wiccan Rede fulfil, an it harm none do what ye will."* In 1974 Lady Gwen Porter published a poem called the "Rede of the Wiccae" which features the familiar Doreen Valiente version beginning "eight words..." The Rede is a moral guideline for Wiccans, but Witches in general have their own personal feelings about the Rede, and may or may not follow it.

Reincarnation – Reincarnation is the belief that a person or animal (being with a soul) is reborn after death. The Soul remains the same, learning in each new lifetime with a new body or form. Some religions believe that you must be a good person and do good deeds during life so you can be reborn in a higher form. Hinduism, Jainism, Buddhism, and Sikhism all believe in reincarnation.

Resurrection – Resurrection is the belief that a being has died and come back from the dead. The most famous examples of resurrection is Jesus Christ; but the Pyramid Texts first recorded the death and resurrection of the god, Osiris, around 2,400 BCE. Other deities that rose form the dead include; Tammuz (Babylonian), Adonis and Dionysus (Greek), and Inanna, (Sumerian). In Norse mythology,

Retrocognition – Retrocognition is the inverse of precognition, and it is the ability to know and perceive past events without having any real means of knowing something. When it comes to retrocognition, it is difficult because the world has been keeping records for a very long time. While you would need specialist knowledge to know something. Saying "I saw Queen Victoria dress in drag and do the hula" would need to be backed up by cotemporary evidence, otherwise it is just someone making an unfounded claim.

Retrograde – Retrograde means "going backwards" and is usually spoken is reference to the Astronomical movements of the planets, and how at certain point in their orbit appear to move backwards. Technically, the planet is not moving in reverse or going backwards, in actuality it has slowed down, and our minds are trying to make sense of this change, so it appears to be moving backwards. It could be called an optical illusion. It is believed that the change of these movements can have an effect on us and our behaviour.

Retrograde Shadow – A retrograde shadow is the periods just before and just after a planet is in Retrograde. These are preparation phases. The Pre-Retrograde Shadow is the preparation for the planet entering retrograde. The Post-Retrograde Shadow is the preparation for the planet moving into its normal motion.

Right-Hand Path – This is a term that refers to people who follow a set of rules, moral codes, doctrine and characteristics, which include things like the Wiccan Rede, Three-Fold Law and Karma. It is a path that is guided by dogma and community beliefs. Those who practice witchcraft may choose to follow this kind of path, but like with all spiritual paths you follow what is right for you, and to adhere to your own morals and ethics.

Ritual – In a literal sense, a ritual is the performance of a ceremonial acts, and in witchcraft and a spiritual sense a ritual is a series of actions which are performed in worship or devotion of deities or special events and celebrations. Examples of rituals include Drawing Down the Moon and Calling the Quarters.

Runes – Runes are two-fold. In one aspect they are letters from a Germanic alphabet, but they are also small stones, clay, wood with the Futhark Runes engraved or painted on them. These Runic letters have their own individual meaning, and can be used in combination with other forms of magic like protection, prosperity, and luck. (See Futhark Runes)

Rune Casting – Rune Casting is a form of divination which uses rune stones to aid in decision making, looking at potential problems and outcomes, but unlike other forms of divination, Runes do not foretell the future, they help to understand the present world and situation you may find yourself in.

S

Sabbat – If we take a surface look at what a Sabbat is, they are festivals and celebration that honour the turning of the Wheel of the Year, but their true meaning goes much deeper. The Sabbats are either associated with the Sun and its path of waxing and waning through the year, or they are agricultural in nature and are associated with the planting and harvesting process. The Solar Festivals include the two equinoxes and solstices; Ostara, Litha, Mabon and Yule. The Agricultural Festivals are Imbolc, Beltane, Lughnasadh and Samhain, and these celebrations fall between the Solar festivals. The Sabbats and the Wheel of the Year is a great circle without start or end, it flows from one to another effortlessly. However, some witches believe that Samhain is the start of the "Witches' New Year", while others believe that Imbolc is the start of the Wheel's cycle. In the Southern Hemisphere, the dates of the festivals are shifted by six months which follows their own seasonal cycle. Samhain – Beltane, Yule – Litha (Solstices), Imbolc – Lughnasadh, Ostara – Mabon. (Equinoxes)

Sacred – When something is sacred, it means that is connected to a deity, or has a spiritual purpose and is worthy of veneration, celebration or worship. What someone considers to be sacred, may not be what another deems to be sacred.

Sacred Space – A Sacred Space is a room, building or space that has been cleansed and protected in order to do magical working. When a witch raises a circle, the space within it is a sacred space. Some witches have a room that is dedicated to their craft and their magical work, and for to others their kitchen is their sacred space, as that is where they do their work.

Sacrifice – In a literal sense Sacrifice is the act of willingly surrendering something that is important to you. Classically when we think of sacrifice, we think about the slaughter of an animal, but for witches today, sacrificing something is a deeply spiritual thing. The purpose of a sacrifice is to make a trade with the gods. If you sacrifice a sheep or goat, the god will bless your crops for another year… though if they aren't pleased, they won't. While some cultures and religions practice animal sacrifice, many witches will choose to sacrifice something like; making donations of food, blood, money or time. It could be going without your favourite takeaway or going out for a fancy meal. It could be something as simple as giving clothes to charity so they can be resold to help others that are in need.

Sage – While Sage is a plant that has long been used by many cultures for cleansing, purifying, wisdom, protection and healing purposes – it's also great in food. There are a number of species of Sage, and from what I know of, they all have the same magical properties. White Sage is sacred to some cultures, but the abundance of species means that another can be used in its place. A Sage is also the male equivalent of the Crone, and is known or sought out for their wisdom, or specialised skills or knowledge.

Salamander – The Salamander is an elemental being that is associated with the Fire element and symbolise immortality, passion, rebirth and the ability to withstand the heat of situations. A Salamander is a species or group of species of amphibian which has an elongated body and stubby limbs.

Samhain – Samhain is one of the festivals in the Wheel of the Year and is pronounced Sow-in. Samhain is a time when the veil between the world of the living and the world of the dead is at its thinnest, and is believed to allow easier communication with Spirits. Samhain is the third and final harvest festival, and this was the time when animals were hunted or slaughtered, and prepared for the long cold months of winter. Samhain is also meaning "Summer's End" and is the halfway point between the Autumn Equinox and the Winter Solstice.

Satanism – Satanism is a group of religious, spiritual and ideological beliefs that are primarily focused on Satan and his worship/veneration. Modern Satanism focuses less on the Devil figure from Christianity, it is rather more focused on personal freedom, personal autonomy and personal responsibility with Satan as a centralised figure. Many Satanists believe that we all have to be responsible for ourselves, and as a liberation from other theistic belief systems. Some who come to Satanism do so as a way to break away from the norm, and mainstream society.

Satanist – A Satanist is someone who worships and venerates Satan. A Satanist is also someone who follows the theistic belief system that has Satan as a central figure, but focus more on personal freedom and liberation.

Saturnalia – Saturnalia is a festival from Ancient Rome which revolved around Saturn (the god of agriculture, prosperity, liberation and time) in December. Saturnalia is a period of merrymaking, drinking, feasting, and the giving of gifts. During Saturnalia, gambling was permitted. The festival lasted for around a week, and is a time when the societal norms of Ancient Rome were turned on their head. It's also been said that all kinds of debauchery took place during this time as well

Scrying – When you are scrying you are using a reflective surface to get messages, revelations, visions and information from Spirit/the Universe/the Divine. It is a form of divination that requires a reflective surface like a crystal ball, a mirror, water, glass or a piece of Obsidian that has been polished really well, even a smart phone can be used as it is a reflective surface when not open. Some mediums choose to do this while in an altered state of consciousness, as they believe that they are able to get clearer and deeper messages.

Séance – A Séance is a meeting, where a group of people have gathered to make contact with the dead, usually though the abilities of a medium. The height of the popularity for Seances was during the mid to late 19th Century, and one of the more famous figures associated with Seances, is Mary Todd Lincoln who held Séances after the loss of her son. It is believed that Abraham Lincoln held a Séance in the White House in 1863, but there is no concrete evidence of this. Today Séances are a popular aspect of Paranormal investigations and by those who seek to prove the existence of ghosts and spirits, but many remain sceptical about how much is suggestion or staged, and what is genuine and real. Those who grieve a loss deeply often find comfort in a séance, because it helps their belief that their loved one's soul lives on beyond physical death.

Seer – A Seer (can be male or female) is someone that is believed to have a supernatural ability to see visions of the future, after which they share these visons with the one who asked them, or to whom they need to be shared with. A Seer can also be called a prophet or an oracle.

Seer Stones – A Seer Stone is a natural stone that has one flat, polished surface, which is believed to hold wisdom, messages or even visions for those that look into it. Nowadays you can buy crystals have been cut and polished to create this flat surface, but the ones that have been naturally polished are the best to reveal its wisdom.

Sex Magic – Sex Magic is a type of magic that uses sexual activity to raise energy during rituals, religious or spiritual practices. Those who practice sex magic as part of their magical practices utilise the unique nature of sexual energy and its potency to fuel their magical work. While the act of sex can be performed, it is not the purpose of the practice, the focus is on the energy that is raised and used during this time. An orgasm is a particularly powerful and potent form of energy which can help manifest dreams and goals into reality.

Shadow Figure – A Shadow Figure is a humanoid-ish shaped black mass, and some people believe that can be benevolent and malevolent in nature. There are a number of schools of thought about what Shadows Figures are, and it largely boils down to what you believe. Sceptics believe they are aspects of someone's psychology, or they are the result as stress, tiredness and generally feeling low. These figures can be found in a number of religions, legends and beliefs from around the world, from the Middle East, Japan and all the way to various Native American beliefs.

Shaman – The Saham is a complex figure and depends on where in the world the Shaman comes from. One common thread is that they are able to gain wisdom, knowledge, healing and divination in the world of Spirit. They are also the people who lead rituals and preserve practices and traditions of their people.

Shamanism – Shamanism is the religious practices that a Shaman leads, and generally Shamanism is characterised by the Shaman connecting to the world of Gods, Spirits, Demons and Ancestors to aids those who follow them. Some spirits are believed to only be responsive with a Shaman, so if I was to try and connect to them, I would have no luck as I am not a Shaman, and I do not have any experience of the beliefs and practices.

Silent Supper – A silent Supper is also known as a Dumb Supper, due to the main aspect is eating a meal in total silence. It is a profound tradition, and brings people together to honour those who have passed, and is observed by many witches all over the world. If you are wanting to hold a Silent Supper, preparation is key as speaking during the event will break the solemnity of the ritual of remembrance.

Sigils – A Sigil is a symbol that has been created for a certain and specific magical reason. Sigils can help to focus the mind on a certain goal by allowing the subconscious "work" while the conscious mind focuses on the symbol that cs been created. Sigils can be used as seals for magical works like spell jars. Sigils can be created by yourself, or you can choose one that someone has created for what you're needing.

Signs – We often ask the Divine, Spirit, or ancestors to send a sign, and these can come to you in many different forms; they can come in dreams, it may be a song you hear, or something you see or smell. If you ask for a sign, then you need to be observant, because they can happen when you least expect it.

Skyclad – When someone is Skyclad, it means they are bare skinned. Some witches believe that wearing clothes can diminish the magical energy that is created during rituals; as they believe that clothes act as a barrier, which prevents connection. On the flipside, some witches have clothes that are only for ritual and spell work. Other witches like myself believe that comfort is key, because being uncomfortable means being distracted, and being distracted during any kind of magical work will diminish the energy raised.

Skull – A Skull is the "head" of any living being which holds the brain, but in the Spiritual World, and magical circles a Skull is a powerful symbol for connecting with the deceased. They can also act as a representation for transition, divinity, gateways to one's ancestors, mortality and the transience of life and nature.

Smoke Cleansing – Smoke Cleansing is the practice of burning herbs, flowers and resins for the purpose of cleansing a space or yourself. Smoke Cleansing is similar to the Native American ceremonial practice of Smudging. With Smoke Cleansing you can add your own preferred herbs, flowers or resins that meet your own needs.

Smudging – This is a practice which has been known as different things, depending on the culture. The most well-known set of practices is from the indigenous Americans. It is a sacred ceremony where sacred herbs are burned for a number of reasons including cleansing and healing. The combination of herbs and practices depend on the specific tribe or nation. In China they have a practice called Moxa, in which dried Mugwort is burned over the various acupuncture points of the body, with Moxa is it believed to bring balance to the Chi/Ki/Qi energy in the body which will allow more effective healing.

Solar – This is a term that refers to something that is related to, associated with or determined by the sun. There are deities from a range of cultures that are associated with the Sun. Lugh, Ra, Surya and Amaterasu are all examples of Solar deities.

Solar Eclipse – A Solar Eclipse occurs when the Moon passes between the Earth and that Sun:

- *Annular Solar Eclipse* – An Annular Solar Eclipse occurs when the Moon passes in front of the visible disk of the Sun and passes through the centre, which causes a ring to occur around the darked area, which is called an Annulus.

This is where the phenomena get its name. The effect is caused because the Moon looks smaller and doesn't fully cover the Sun.

- *Hybrid Solar Eclipse* – A Hybrid Eclipse is a rare occurrence when the Moon progresses across the Sun and changes from an Annular Solar Eclipse to a Total Solar Eclipse.
- *Partial Solar Eclipse* – A Partial Solar Eclipse is when only part of the Moon obscures the Sun's visible disk. During a Partial Solar Eclipse, the daytime light is not affected.
- *Total Solar Eclipse* – A Total Eclipse occurs when the Moon completely covers the surface of the Sun that's viewable from Earth. Normally a Total Solar Eclipse can be seen from a limited area, and anyone out of that zone may be able to see a Partial Eclipse. During a Total Solar Eclipse, the daytime sky may be darkened.

Solstice – A Solstice occurs twice a year and marks the times when the Sun is either at its most northern or southern point from the equator, and is either at its highest or lowest point in the sky. When it is the Summer Solstice in the Northern Hemisphere, it is the Winter Solstice in the Southern Hemisphere and vice versa.

- *Summer Solstice* – During the Summer Solstice one of the Earth's poles is at its most extreme angle towards the Sun, which causes the Sun to be the highest in the sky, the hours of daylight are at their longest too.
- *Winter Solstice* – During the Winte Solstice one of the Earth's poles is at its most extreme angle away from the Sun, which causes the Sun to be at its lowest point in the sky, the hours of daylight are at their shortest.

Solitary Witch – Being a Solitary Witch means you do things alone, or you prefer to practice on your own. As Witches it's not always possible to be part of a coven or community for whatever reason, so they practice on their own. Some of the spells and rituals in the plethora of books and online resources can be designed for groups and covens, as a Solitary you can adapt and adjust any spell to work with just your own energy.

So, Mote it Be – The origin of "So mote it be" may surprise you because it is believed that the Freemasons were the first to use the phrase, and the earliest document in the UK was from the 15th century. It's role in Freemasonry and modern Pagan and Witch circles is essentially the same. It was used at the end of a prayer or ritual, and later spells, how Amen is used in Christian Prayers. It's used as a way to denote that the ritual or magical work has come to an end. Other versions include; "and so shall it be" or "as I will it, so it shall be" or something as simple as "this is my will, so it shall be."

Soul – The Soul is an immaterial or spiritual part of a living being, and is often seen as immortal. Some believe that after death the Soul goes to another place like Heaven or Valhalla, or to somewhere like Tartarus. While others believe that the soul is reborn into another form so they can attain enlightenment and Nirvana. In the Witch, Pagan and Spiritual communities' people will hold their own view of the Soul and what happens to it after the body has died.

Soul Family – The term Soul Family, refers to the group of souls that you meet lifetime after lifetime, and over those lifetimes you have become friends. This happens on a non-physical level, and as you progress through your soul's lifetime you will experience life on many levels, this physical life you're living is just one of many. A Soul Family generally consists of seven souls that have chosen long before this life to be together. They don't always incarnate together, but when you meet a member of your Soul Family, you feel as if you have come "home", and you feel safe on a level you've not felt before. Your Soul Family is always there for you...no matter what. Those of your Soul Family that have not been incarnated often become Spirit Guides and Guardians to the one on the physical plane.

Soul Mate – The term Soul Mate often refers to someone you have an inexplicable connection with another. It is a connection that happens the moment you meet, and you can't explain why or how it happened, but you can't deny the connection. There are two schools of thought on soul mates. The first school of thought is that you only have a single Soul Mate, and it is a romantic partner due to the intensity and depth of connection. The other school of thought is that you have many Soul Mates in your life, and they come and go throughout your life, and they act as teachers, guides, mentors or simply as a person that supports you with no questions asked. The deep relationships that form through a soul connection can be very challenging for both people, and the whole point of this kind of relationship is to act as a mirror and to show you how to be yourself.

Sour Jar – A Sour Jar is a form of spell that is designed to sour someone's life, and to make things turn upside down for them. This is usually done in the form of a jar, with a range of ingredients that are believed to have baneful properties. The jar can either use wet or dry ingredients, or a combination of both.

Spell – In a literal sense, a Spell is a set of words and/or actions that are designed to create a specific outcome. When you are working with spells, you are seeking to alter a situation by either introducing new energy or by rearranging the energy that is already present in the situation. When you perform a spell, you do so with awareness and intent to bring about change. Spells are a sequence of actions that are performed on a physical level to create change on a different level.

Sprite – Sprite is another term that can be used to refer to a Faerie, an elf or other mythical faerie-like creature. Naiads, Nereids and Sirens are all type of water sprites. A Nixie is actually a Germanic water Sprite that has characteristics in common with mermaids and sirens.

Spirit – The Spirit is something that is intangible in nature, it can't be held or calculated, but it is something that all of us intuitively know about. Spirit actually has a few different definitions when it comes to witchcraft:

1. Spirit is another name for the Soul, and is the spiritual part of someone's being.
2. Spirit can also be another name for a ghost or spectre.
3. Spirits (aka alcohol) can also be used in various traditions and practices.
4. Spirit or Akasha is the element that sits at the top point of a pentagram, or in certain Wiccan traditions is considered to sit at the centre of the compass.

Spoony Magic – Spoony Magic isn't a technical term for a form of magical practices, but it is one that has been popping up on social media in recent years. Spoony Magic is something that is practiced by someone who has a chronic illness or disability that impacts how they practice.

Staff – A Staff is a long stick that is used to give support while walking or climbing. It can also be used as a weapon, but that isn't really the role it plays in Witchcraft. In relation to Witchcraft a Staff can be used in a similar way to a wand as it can channel energy, dispel energy and can help to mark boundaries on the ground. Staves are also part of the standard tarot deck which can symbolise wisdom, strength, passions, and drive.

Stregheria – This is an archaic term from Italy that literally means 'witchcraft'. Those who did follow this path venerated and worshipped the Lunar Goddess and Horned God which stem from the Etruscan deities and ancestral spirits. Today Italians use the word 'Stregoneria' to refer to witchcraft.

Subtle Body – A Subtle Body is a term used to refer to the non-physical aspects of a person. This includes their emotions, their mind, their memories. One key aspect of a Subtle Body is that is not physical, nor is it spiritual in nature. I have also seen the term Subtle Bodies relate to the Aura and its layers.

Subtle Magic – Subtle Magic is something that refers to magic that is unseen, and while something is unseen it doesn't mean it won't have an effect on something or someone.

Succubus – A Succubus is a female demon or a malicious spirit or entity that seduces men through their dreams in order to have physical relations with them while they sleep. A Succubus relies on these sexual interactions with men to survive, but if a bond is formed it is believed that she will drain men of their vitality and virility. The male version of a Succubus is an Incubus.

Summerland – The Summerland is a concept of the afterlife, and is a place that Theosophists believed good souls went to after death. This term has been adopted by Wiccans and other modern Pagans of varying kinds. It is essentially another name for Heaven, the Elysian Fields etc...

Supernatural – Supernatural is something that happens which seems to be beyond human and scientific understanding. This could be something that happens to you – like seeing a spirit or shadow figure, or even having a gift like Clairvoyance is supernatural in nature as it is something that isn't directly found in nature. Another term that is interlinked with supernatural is paranormal.

Superstition – A superstition is a widely held belief but can be completely irrational, and not really based in any truth or fact. Not walking under a ladder. Breaking a mirror will bring bad luck. Stepping on a crack will break a person's back. If a black cat crosses your path, it is bad luck. None of these have any rational truth.

Sweet Jar – A Sweet Jar is the opposite in nature to the Sour Jar, as this one works towards sweetening someone. You can use it for sweetening someone's personality and disposition, or it can be used to affect how someone sees you, and has them thinking of you in a more positive light. In this jar you would use sweet things like sugars, honey, syrups, treacle; basically, anything that is extremely sweet. If you don't get the feeling, that you could buy your dentist a new car with the amount of sugary and sweet things, then it's not sweet enough.

Sword – A sword is a long blade, similar to a dagger or knife, just bigger and longer. The Sword symbolises power, and is primarily used in Ceremonial Magic/High Magic and initiations into various practices. The sword is a phallic and masculine symbol and the sheath is a yoni and feminine symbol, so it is another representation of the Great Rite and union of the male and female. In Tarot Swords represent the intellect, but they also represent action, courage, ambition and conflicts.

Sylph – The Sylph is an Air elemental or spirit. Some consider that Sylphs are member of the Fae, while others see them as being demons. One thing that is different from other Elementals spirits, a Sylph is mortal and can die from a range of things like illness and injury to dying of starvation.

Sympathetic Magic – Sympathetic magic is a type of magic that uses a representation or symbol, and whatever happens to that representation is believed to have the same effect on whatever it represents. The best example of this is a Poppet. You create a doll out of whatever material you like, and you infuse it with herbs, crystals and oils which all correspond to your intention. These aspects and spoken words of intention can be used for a range of things from healing to something more baneful. In popular and fictional media, the "Voodoo Doll" is a type of sympathetic magic

Synchronicities – Synchronicities are the simultaneous events that appear to be related because there is no other apparent reason for them to be connected otherwise. It's as if events happen at the same time because some greater force has planned them that way.

T

Taglock – Taglock refers to aspects of witchcraft that use anatomical ingredients like blood, spit, hair, nail clippings; basically, anything that comes from a person's body and contains DNA. A Taglock has been used in various aspects of witchcraft for a very long time, and I mean a very, very long time. Using these kinds of ingredients is not inherently baneful or malevolent, they are simply a way of creating a powerful bond, which means they can be used for protection and healing. Nowadays there are ways of getting these kinds of ingredients which do not include the person offering them. Used tissues, discarded utensils, cigarette butts.

Talisman – A Talisman is an object that is believed to protect against evil and malevolent forces, but they are also used to attract luck, abundance and general good things. Talismans are usually carried (in pockets, in handbags etc) but they can be installed in places permanently.

Tantra – Tantra is an Eastern practice with its roots in Hinduism and Buddhism. Tantra means "woven together" and people who practice Tantra weave the physical and spiritual together. During the sexual experience Tantra teaches that there is importance in the intimacy, and the aim of the practice isn't to achieve orgasm, it is more about the connection and the energy between you.

Tarot – Tarot is a form of divination which has 78 cards and is split into two groups; the Major Arcana and the Minor Arcana. Tarot helps to navigate your spiritual path though being aware of yourself and what is happening around you. There is no right or wrong way to read tarot cards, and while each card has a traditional meaning, it is up to the reader to interpret what the card is saying in relation to the cards around it.

Tea Leaf Reading – Tea Leaf Reading is also known as Tasseography, and is a form of divination and fortune telling which involves looking at the shapes made from steeping tea. The patterns and shapes that are made all have a meaning and it is believed that they can foretell the future. *This only work with loose teas, as tea bags prevent the tea from being left behind in the cup.*

Telepathy – Telepathy is an ability that people believe you can hear the thoughts of others; and can communicate with them without using their voice. Telepathy comes under the category of ESP and Psychic.

Thaumaturgy – Thaumaturgy is the practice of magic which is designed to change the physical world through ritual. Some consider this to be akin to working miracles through rituals and incantations.

Theban Script – Theban Script is also known as the "Witch's Alphabet". It is a Latin-based alphabet which has been used as a way to 'hide' information. It has been popular with Wiccans and other practitioners because they can hide their Book of Shadows in plain sight.

Threefold Law – The Threefold Law is also known as the 'Rule of Three' and 'Law of Return' and they all boil down to the belief that whatever you send out to the Universe/World will come back to you three times, and this applies to positive and negative things. Not everyone in the Spiritual and Witchy community follows this 'law', but practice in accordance to their own principles and ethics.

The Great Work – The Great Work is believed to the pinnacle of Alchemy, the Magnum Opus, the creation of the Philosopher's Stone, a formula which was believed to turn base metals into gold.

Theology – Theology is the study of religion, faith and their practices. Some believe that it is only about the study of 'God', but it is about more than just that, it can be expanded to be the study of religion and belief itself. It is essentially the study and search for religious truth.

Theosophy – Theosophy was established in the 19th Century America, and is a religious and philosophical system that has a mystical way of thinking about the world. The practitioners believe that there is a deeply spiritual way to live and often practice contemplation.

Theurgy – Theurgy is the belief that the supernatural or divine forces have power and influence over everyday life.

Tincture – A Tincture is a medicine or remedy where ingredients have been soaked or dissolved in alcohol. It is possible to make tinctures at home without any fancy equipment.

Tonic – A Tonic is something that makes you feel better, or feels like it is restoring your vitality and vigour. It is usually a drink of some kind made from herbs and flowers.

Totem – A Totem is an object or animal that is believed to have spiritual significance and has been adopted as a symbol or emblem. In the world of Witches, Totems are generally animals that have appeared in your life and is aiding you with something in your life. Some totems stay with you while you are going through situations and challenges, while some stay with you for your whole life. Totems are originally from Ojibwe Native American people, but it has been adopted by many who follow a spiritual path.

Tradition – Traditions are beliefs and customs that have been passed down from generation to generation. It is also used to describe the different forms of a belief system. Alexandrian Wicca and Gardnerian Wicca are two different traditions of Wicca.

Traditional Witchcraft – Traditional Witchcraft is a broad term that is associated with the various Neo-Pagan practices. Some consider Traditional Witchcraft an older way of practicing than Wicca, and may even reject the Gardnerian Wicca tradition.

Trance – A Trance is a state where you are only semi-conscious and it is characterised by the person in the trance being oblivious or unaware of what is happening around them. Trances can be induced by meditation, hypnosis or with the use of mind-altering substances. These Trance states are temporary and the person with come round given enough time.

Transcendent – When you experience something Transcendent, you are experiencing something that is beyond the normal experiences you have as a human. You surpass what you have experienced before, but it may not be something that is permanent. It can be something temporary, but they can be life changing events.

Tree of Life – The Tree of Life represents the connection between the Earth, Heaven and the afterlife in general. Its roots reach deep as the branches reach for the sun. Over the years it has come to represent a multitude of things from enlightenment, wisdom, spiritual growth to resilience, longevity and how all life is interconnected. For some it is the source of all life, and is the force that connects us all to one another, to the past, the future and the cycle of birth, life, death and rebirth.

Trinity – A Trinity is a group of three figures, or three aspects of a divine figure. In Christianity there is Father, Son and Holy Spirit, but trinities have been part of other cultures too, but some trinities are called a Triad. Here are some other examples of Trinities from other cultures.

- In Hinduism they have a trinity called Trimurti where the three figures are Brahma (creator), Vishnu (preserver) and Shiva (destroyer).
- In Ancient Greece Hecate was often depicted as three figures in one. They represent the various aspects of Hecate and how her influence spread to the earth, sea and heavens. In later periods she became a triple goddess that stood back-to-back so she could see in all direction at one, as she is deeply connected to the crossroads.
- In Celtic Mythology the fearsome Morrigan was represented as a trinity, or having three aspects to her being. These aspects may shift a little and are a little inconsistent. She sometimes features as one of the daughters of Ernmas: Babd, Macha and Morrigan, or she is part of a trinity with Babd, and Anand.

Triple Goddess – The Triple Goddess is a figure (or figures) that feature in a number of modern Pagan traditions, where three different and distinct aspects are represented in one being. The Morrigan and Brigid are two popular figures that appear as a Triple Goddess. In Hinduism there is a comparative figure called Tridevi which refers to the three supreme goddesses of Hinduism, Lakshmi, Saraswati and Parvati/Kali.

Triple Moon – The Triple Moon is a popular symbol in the Pagan and Witchy world as it represents the passages of the Moon's phases but it also honours the divine aspects of womanhood from a Maiden through her life to becoming a crone. It is drawn as a full moon at the centre with a crescent moon either side

Tuning Fork – A tuning fork is a metal instrument used by musicians, which when struck gives of a specific note or pitch. In a spiritual sense their tone and vibrations can stimulate the Qi/Chi/Ki within the body and helps the body's energy to flow naturally. It is believed that different frequencies have different healing properties and effects on the body.

Twin Flame – The Twin Flame is a concept where two people are so deeply connected that it is as if they feel like they are part each other. They act as a mirror for each other, they are the one who can show you the truest reflect of yourself. It is believed that you feel this way because your soul is being mirrored, and you feel it in every cell of your being. It's not just the good aspects that are reflected, it is the good, the bad and the ugly. With your Twin Flame you can work through things you fear but haven't been able to with anyone else. Unlike Soul Mates, there is only one twin flame because it is believed that when your soul was born it split into two, to learn all it can before finding the other half. When it finds it the soul has learned all it can and will now return to the Source.

U

Umbra – The Umbra is the part of a shadow in which all light from a given source is excluded. The areas most affected by the Umbra will experience a Total Eclipse.

Uncrossing – To 'uncross' something in witchcraft, you are working towards unblocking and releasing energies and situations which may prevent forward movements to reaching your goals. When you work on Uncrossing Spells and rituals, you are working to push back anything that is stopping you externally; you are also working on releasing negative emotions that you are holding.

Underworld – The Underworld is a complicated concept, as not all versions of the underworld is a place of evil or where bad people go after death. For many world mythologies it is a place where all souls reside, good or bad. In Greek Mythology the realm of Hades was home to Elysium (a heaven-like place where special souls and heroes live), the Asphodel Meadows (where the average soul lives) and the infamous Tartarus where the damned souls go to be punished, it is also were several of the Titans are imprisoned. In Welsh mythology the underworld or otherworld is known as Annwn, and is a place where the soul is eternally young, there is no disease, and where food is abundant, thanks to the Cauldron of Plenty.

Undine – An Undine is an elemental Spirit associated with water. They love to inhabit waterfalls, mountain or meadow pools, and have enchanting singing voices. Undine is also a category which species like Mermaids and Naiads fall under.

Unverifiable Personal Gnosis (UPG) – Unverifiable Personal Gnosis refers to a belief that someone has that has been adopted through personal experience, and for them it is true for their spiritual journey, but is not held by others. Unverifiable means that the beliefs have not been able to be verified or accepted by the general community or people across the world. Those who follow a Spirit-led path often have beliefs that aren't easily proven.

Universe – The easiest way to describe what the Universe is, is simply, it is everything. It is what all matter belongs to, it is the cosmos, and all its energies. The Universe is so big, and so vast that the human mind can't truly understand its size or age; the number are just too big.

Universal Consciousness – This is a metaphysical concept which states that there is an underlying essence or thread that unites all beings, and share a pool of wisdom. While is popular in modern religious belief or spiritual practices, the concept has been around since the 5th Century BCE.

V

Valkyrie – A Valkyrie is a female figure in Norse Mythology and whose name means "Chooser of the Fallen". Their role was to scour the battlefields for those who are worthy to grace the halls of Odin (Valhalla) and Freyja (Sessrúmnir). They are also known to be the handmaids of Odin, especially when no battles are being fought.

Vampire – A Vampire is a creature of folklore which was a reanimated body of the dead, they leave their graves during the night to drink the blood of humans – usually from the neck, leaving fang marks behind. Vampires have long been seen as being associated with the dead bodies of witches, suicide victims and all manner of evil spirits.

Vanir – The Vanir are the other group of gods in Norse mythology who held sway over and responsible for fertility, wisdom, foresight and wealth. The Vanir are allied with the Aesir, but often appear to be subordinate or answer to them. Njord, the god of the sea and wind was the leader of the Vanir gods.

Veiling – Veiling is the act of covering your head or body for religious or spiritual practices. Some cultures use veiling or the act of covering your head as an act of devotion. In the spiritual and witchcraft world, the act of veiling is practiced with covering and protecting the crown from negative and unwanted energies. Veiling as a witch is not required, but it's fine if you feel like you are being drawn to do so.

Vesica Piscis –A Vesica Piscis is a shape in geometry, which is formed when two circles of the same size are drawn with the centre of each circle, sitting on the other's circumference.

The most famous display of this shape is at Chalice Well in Glastonbury, England. In spiritual circles it represents the various types of Goddess energy, and can be used as a symbol to attract more feminine energy into your practice. It is also a symbol that is associated with the balancing of energies during your own magical workings.

Vibration – The literal meaning of vibration is described as the movement of particles which create a point of equilibrium. In a spiritual and metaphysical sense, we are talking about the subtle vibrations, the movement of the atoms in the universe. When you exist and vibrate at a higher frequency it means that person has a positive attitude and is at peace with their lives. When you exist and vibrate at a lower frequency it means that person doesn't have a positive attitude and may have a "why me" or victim mentality.

Vision Quest – Vision Quests are tied intricately with some Native American and Indigenous people, and is an important rite of passage for people of these communities. Usually taken around the start of puberty, where the participant attempts to get visions of the guardian spirit they will have later in life. A Vision Quest is an experience that goes beyond everyday experiences. It is a mystical journey where the person searches for their guardian; these spirits are sometimes as an animal with human qualities and characteristics.

Visualisation – Visualisation in a literal sense is where you create the image of something in your mind. Through visualisation a witch can work on manifesting something by keeping it clear in their minds-eye. One way you can say it, is that it is the ability to use the full power of your imagination and creativity to experience reality differently.

Void of Course – The concept of Void of Course describes the time when the Moon has no major aspects before it moves into another sign. It is a term that relates to the transitioning of the Moon from one astrological sign into another. Over the last few years there has been a debate over whether Void of Course has any impact on our lives. As Void of Course is a time when nothing really happens; it can be an ideal time to get organised without the influence from the signs or the planets.

Voodoo – Voodoo or Vodou is a religion that has its roots in African ancestral worship and has been practiced in various places in the Caribbean like Haiti. In the southern parts of America practitioners have blended Ancestral worship with the veneration of Catholic figures like angels and saints. As a religion Voodoo/Vodou have a set of religious and long-established practices and traditions, and is a way of life for its followers and practitioners.

Voodoo Doll – A Voodoo Doll is a small figure made in the likeness of someone that has been created for a specific purpose. They are created and used in the same way a Poppet is. It is believed that whatever happens to the doll, happens to the person it's a likeness of. A Voodoo Doll, like the Poppet is a form of sympathetic magic.

W

Wand – A wand is a stick or rod which can be used for a wide range of magic. The main role of the Wand today is to direct, guide and channel energy towards a goal or magical intention. You can use a wand to 'draw' a ritual circle, or magical symbols or sigils in the air.

Warlock – The term Warlock has gone through many changes over the years, some sources say that Warlock means "Oath Breaker" or "deceiver" and does magic only for their own or evil purposes. Nowadays, the term Warlock has started to be used in reference to male witches, and male practitioners of the craft.

Water – One of the four fundamental elements of nature, along with Air, Earth and Fire. It is what provides our connection to the physical world.

Water Sign – When someone is born under the Water element, they are said to be intuitive, emotional, empathetic and has a strong connection to the emotional, mental and spiritual aspects of life. These people tend to be introverted and seek knowledge and understanding. They prefer to remain in the background as someone supporting others. The Water signs are Cancer, Scorpio and Pisces.

Water (types of) – Water is one of the fundamental elements, but it is also the most adaptable element and can not only carry its own properties, it can be collected, charged or infused to enhance its properties.

- *Colour Water* – This is water that can been charged in a coloured bottle or glass and has been infused with the properties of whatever colour you desire.
- *Crystal Water* – This is water than has been charged and infused with crystals, and it is believed that the properties of the crystals. *I would never recommend you put crystals into water, but you can infuse water indirectly by placing crystals around the glass or bottle.*
- *Dew* – Dew is the water that has gathered on exposed surfaces when water vapour has condensed. You can usually find Dew on plants and grass in the morning. Dew can be used for: healing, beauty and glamour magic, eyesight, love, tranquillity, cleansing and working with the Fae.
- *Holy Water* – Usually Holy water has been blessed by a priest, but in witchcraft it has been blessed with herbs, oils and salts. Like all forms of Holy Water, it can be used for banishing, cleansing and purification.
- *Lake/Pond Water* – Lake/Pond Water is collected from a lake or pond and can be used for; peace, joy, self-discovery and reflection and for relaxation purposes.
- *Moon Water* – Moon Water has been charged under a certain phase of the Moon – typically it is the Full Moon and can be used for; cleansing, blessing and charging items, it can be used in bath rituals, healing, empowering spells. They can also be used in baneful magic.
- *Rain Water* – Rain Water has been collected while it is raining and can be used for; growth spells, rebirth and renewal, cleansing, scrying and ritual baths.
- *River water* – River Water is collected from a river and can be used for; moving forward, warding, breakthroughs, power and charging items.
- *Sea Water* – Sea Water has been collected from the sea, and because it is naturally salted it is perfect for cleansing,

banishing, protection, manifestation, healing rituals and providing emotional balance.

- *Solar Water* – Solar (Sun) Water has been left in the sunlight for a set period of time, and can be used for; invigoration, protection, happiness, creativity, fertility and protection.
- *Spring Water* – Spring Water is collected from natural springs and can be used for; growth, cleansing, abundance, manifestation and in beauty and glamour magic. *Please note, that this does not include bottled spring water.*
- *Snow Water* – Snow Water is snow that has been collected and allowed to thaw into water. When you collect the Snow will depend on how the Snow Water will act. If you collect it from a snow storm, it will act quickly, and if you collect it from the ground or gentle flurries it will act at a gentler pace. Snow Water can be used for; unthawing situations to break down barriers, transformation, balance, peace and transitions.
- *Storm Water* – Storm Water has been collected during a storm, and can be used for; vitality, self-esteem, confidence, courage, strength, protection or to add oomph to a spell. Storms tend to be high energy times, and this high energy transfers to water that has been collected.
- *Swamp/Bog Water* – Swamp/Bog Water has been collected from a more stagnant water source, and as such holds the energies of the environment and blend the water and earth elements. Swamp Water can be used for spells that need to slow things down, to muddy a situation or place something in a space of stillness.
- *War Water* – War Water is primarily used in Hoodoo and from what I have found used to create discord, mayhem and can be used in a plethora of baneful magic spells and rituals.

Wavelength – A Wavelength is literally the distance between two points of identical waves of energy. Wavelengths can be associated to the visual colour spectrum (light) and in soundwaves. Wavelength can be used to refer to a group of people who have the same ideas, beliefs, or agree on something.

Web Weaving – This is a term that I've only come across a few times and while it may have a few different meanings (often related to the internet), what I have discovered is that Web Weavers create their own spells, and tend not to write them down as they rely on the unique nature of the energy at the time of the spell. It is believed that while many witches are restricted through correspondences and what they have learned, Web Weavers tend to go with their own flow and can be seen as "winging it".

Wheel of the Year – The Wheel of the Year is the annual cycle of the seasons, and the festivals associated with the seasons. The Wheel represents the ebb and flow of light and dark in the year, and how they hold sway over our lives and practices. The eight festivals of the Wheel are known as Sabbats and are either solar or agricultural in nature. While the Wheel of the Year conceptualises celebrations while may have been held from the past, the Wheel as we know it today was primarily developed by the pioneers of the modern Pagan, Wiccan and Witchcraft movements in the mid-20th Century.

White Magic – White Magic is the polar opposite of "Black" magic, while the latter focuses on baneful of self-absorbed magics, the former focuses on healing, protecting and bringing peace and prosperity to all.

Wicca – Wicca is a modern, Earth-centred religion, whose worship is focused on the Goddess and the Horned God.

Wicca was developed in the 1950's by Gerald Gardner and his followers. He was initiated into the New Forest Witches Coven in 1939, from which he learned what would one day become Wicca. Wiccan's follow the Wiccan Rede which is a moral code of conduct which boils down to "as long as you don't harm anyone, do whatever you want".

Widdershins – Widdershins refers to a movement which goes against the Sun's natural path, so counterclockwise (or anti-clockwise). When you move in a Widdershins direction you are banishing something. When raising a Circle for rituals, you do so by moving clockwise because you are raising the energy. Once the ritual is over, to release the circle, you move in an anti-clockwise.

Wild Hunt – The Wild Hunt is a myth from the North-Eastern reaches of Europe concerning an epic hunting party of spectres led by the Norse god Odin, or a hero from Norse Mythology. The Hunt kidnaps any mortal that has not found a hiding place when the Hunt rides through; any mortal abducted is taken to the underworld. The Wild Hunt rides during the deepest darkest nights of the Winter months. In some areas of Europe, the arrival of the Hunt was a herald of misfortunes like wars, plagues or famines.

Wise Woman – A Wise Woman is someone who has dedicated her life to helping, healing and learning. She is knowledgeable about herbs, charms and traditional lore that she has learned through her life. She is nurturing, kind, a teacher and a faithful friend, but she won't allow anyone to take advantage of her kindness, as traditionally when one visited a Wise Woman, a gift would be given for her time, or as payment for her services.

Witch – This is one of those terms with a plethora of meanings, and not all of them are pleasant. One definition refers to a hag, an old woman who is ugly or deformed. However, a Witch is someone that has a deep and abiding love and connection to the physical and spiritual world, it is like they have one foot in each, so they can be truly connected. A Witch doesn't need to belong to any religion to practice their craft.

Witch's Ball – A Witch's Ball is a hollow spherical vessel which is believed to trap evil or baneful energies, while protecting the space in which it is hung. You can make a Witch's ball nowadays by getting the "make your own bauble" kits and fill them with whatever herbs, spices and crystals that will work towards your intention.

Witch's' Bell – The Witch's' Bell is a bell (or multiple bells) that is hung over the door to your home, or near it. The sound the bells make are believed to banish anything that could be harmful to you and your home. You can also use them to stir up stagnant energy, and get it moving again.

Witch's' Ladder – A Witch's Ladder is a folk practice which involves weaving a spell by knotting hair or chords. The number of knots used is determined by what your intentions are, which will have an effect on the outcome. Some witches believe that the cord needs to be hidden somewhere safe, but this is a personal preference.

Witchling – This is a term that has been floated around the Witchy world for a while, and it is one that I use regularly. A Witchling is child that has an interest in the craft, and strives to learn and know all they can

Witchcraft – If we strip everything away, at its core Witchcraft is simply a way of practicing your beliefs. There are no requirements to believe in one thing to another, and some witches do not believe in any divine force. Historically witchcraft was seen as evil and those who practiced this kind of magic were shunned and/or killed for their knowledge, but today you are more than likely going to find a witch seeking balance and harmony, although some will use baneful magic in order to attain their goal.

Witch Doctor – A Witch Doctor has a number of roles in their communities. They are the doctors, the magicians and the priests, they are the teachers, protectors and healers. They lean heavily into the folkloric beliefs of their communities, and can divine for insight and wisdom. *This is a very basic view of what a witch doctor is, when in reality their role is nuanced, and would take longer to explore than I have the ability to convey here.*

Witching Hour – The Witching Hour refers to a time during the night that is associated with spiritual and supernatural events occur. There are two schools of thought about when the Witching hour is; one group believe that midnight is the start of the witching hour, while the other believes that the Witching hour is between 3 and 4 am. It is believed that performing magic during this time can amplify the energies you are calling on. It is a point during the night when it is as it's darkest. If you are a Nocturnal practitioner, this would be the time to work your magic.

Witch Trials – A Witch Trial is where someone (male or female) was put on trial because they were believed to be a witch. Often those accused would end up dead from either the method used to extract a confession, or they were killed. This "craze" began in Europe and spread quickly to all corners of the continent, and even followed the Pilgrims to the Americas. One of the most infamous Witch Trials took place in Salem village in 1692. Another famous one was the Pendle Witch Trials in England in 1612.

Wizard – When I think of a Wizard, Merlin, and Gandalf come to mind, as they are powerful beings with great magical skills. A Wizard is a man who practices magic, and who has a deep and vast wealth of knowledge and wisdom. They often hold role of councillor or advisor to others – like Merlin to King Arthur or Nestor of the Iliad.

World Tree – The most famous World Tree is Yggdrasil, a colossal tree with branches that reach high into the sky, while its roots grow deep. The World Tree, or sacred trees feature in cultures all over the world but they all carry a common thread and theme, they represent the continuous cycle of life, death, rebirth and how all life, regardless of its plane of existence is connected.

Wyrd – This is a concept that feature primarily in folklore associated with Beowulf, and it refers to the powerful forces that have control over the lives of mortals. It could be called, fate, destiny or the doom of man. It is also associated with a trio of sisters who measure the life of men and gods, and determine when their lives end. These three are known as the Wyrd Sisters (it's not just a Terry Pratchett book) or the Norn. They have a similar role to the Fates from Ancient Greece.

X

Yin & Yang – Yin and Yang are part of a Chinese philosophy which state that these forces are both complimentary and interconnected. Yin represents all that is feminine and is associated with passivity, things that are small, cold and soft. Yang is its opposite force, so Yang represents all that is masculine and is associated with activity and things that are big, warm and hard. In Paganism and Witchcraft, the concept of Yin & Yang represents the balance and interplay of these opposing forces. Yin and Yang can help a witch to explore aspects of magic, which they would not normally. In witchcraft Yin represents subtle magics of the mental aspect of spellcasting while Yang represents the more forceful magics or the physical aspect of spellcasting.

Yggdrasil – Yggdrasil is the sacred Ash tree from Norse Mythology, and it is the branches of this tree that holds the nine worlds of the cosmos. The branches of Yggdrasil reach high into the heavens and are supported by three enormous roots which spread far out from the tree. Within its branches are the nine worlds including Asgard (home of the Aesir gods), Midgard (home of humanity), Vanaheim (home of the Vanir gods), Jötunheim (home of the giants) and Helheim (the land of the dead/underworld.

Youth – In simple terms the Youth is the male counterpart to the Crone/Maiden. He is full of promise, potential and energy. They are associated with the Spring months and the fertility that embodies. He is virile, powerful but also impulsive.

Yule – Yule is the festival which celebrates the start of Winter and is the Winter Solstice. The date of the solstice varies and

Y

Yin & Yang – Yin and Yang are part of a Chinese philosophy which state that these forces are both complimentary and interconnected. Yin represents all that is feminine and is associated with passivity, things that are small, cold and soft. Yang is its opposite force, so Yang represents all that is masculine and is associated with activity and things that are big, warm and hard. In Paganism and Witchcraft, the concept of Yin & Yang represents the balance and interplay of these opposing forces. Yin and Yang can help a witch to explore aspects of magic, which they would not normally. In witchcraft Yin represents subtle magics or the mental aspect of spellcasting; while Yang represents the more forceful magics or the physical aspect of spellcasting.

Yggdrasil – Yggdrasil is the sacred Ash tree from Norse Mythology, and it is the branches of this tree that holds the nine worlds of the Cosmos. The branches of Yggdrasil reach high into the heavens, and are supported by three immense roots which reach far from the tree. Within its branches are the nine worlds including Asgard (home of the Aesir gods), Midgard (home of humanity), Vanaheim (home of the Vanir gods), Jötunheim (home of the giants) and Helheim (the land of the dead/underworld.

Youth – In simple terms the Youth is the male counterpart to the female Maiden. He is full of promise, potential and energy. They are associated with the Spring months and the fertility that it embodies. He is virile, powerful but also impulsive.

Yule – Yule is the festival which celebrates the start of Winter and is the Winter Solstice. The date of the solstice varies due to the orbiting of the Earth around the sun. During Yule, the Earth's axis points away from the sun, which means the sun is at it's lowest point in the sky, leading to the shortest day of the year. The celebrations of Yule have been absorbed and adapted over the centuries, especially with the spread of Christianity. Most cultures have some kind of celebration around the the Winter Solstice. Saturnalia from Ancient Rome, the Dong Zhi of China, and the Yalda festival of Persia are all examples of celebrations around the Winter Solstice.

Yule Log – A Yule Log is a log that has been specially chosen to be burnt in the hearth during the Winter Solstice. Once the log has been lit, it needs to burn through because to light it again is seen as unlucky. The lighting and burning of the Yule Log in the hearth, symbolises the rebirth of the Sun, and its growing strength. Some cultures believed that burning the Yule Log would drive away evil spirits throughout the winter months.

Z

Zen – We often think than Zen is simply a state of peace and balance, but as part of Mahayana Buddhism it goes far beyond just balance and peace. It places value in the act of meditation and intuition. Those who choose to find their "Zen" are choosing to slow their life down so they can focus on meditation.

Zodiac "the" – If we look at the literal meaning of what the zodiac is, it refers to a group of twelve constellations which the Sun passes through throughout the year. The sun spends around four weeks in each constellation, or sign, and these signs are believed to have deep meanings and influence over humanity. The signs are; Aries, Taurus, Gemini, Cancer, Leo, Virgo, Libra, Scorpio, Sagittarius, Capricorn, Aquarius, Pisces. Aries is often believed to be the first sign of the Zodiac, beginning in March and Pisces is the last sign, which ends just before Aries begins.

Bibliography

Bookshelf

Hedgewitch by Rae Beth
Moonology by Yasmin Boland
Buckland's Complete Companion of Witchcraft by Raymond Buckland
Wicca: Moon Magic by Lisa Chamberlain
Wicca: Herbal Magic by Lisa Chamberlain
The Chakra Project by Georgia Coleridge
Numerology by Richard Craze
Norse Magic by D.J Conway
Earth, Air, Fire Water by Scott Cunningham
Wicca: A Guide for the Solitary Practitioner by Scott Cunningham
Living Wicca by Scott Cunningham
A Complete Guide to Magic and Ritual by Cassandra Eason
Earth Magic by Steven D. Farmer
A Witches' Bible by Janet and Stewart Farrar
Sage Burning by Kiera Fog
Way of the Goddess by Ann-Marie Gallagher
Astrology and Horoscopes by Geddes and Grosset
Astrology Bible by Judy Hall
The Language of Flowers by Mandy Kirby
Solitary Wicca: For Life by Arin Murphy-Hiscock
Hoodoo: Folk Magic by Rachel Patterson
The Way of Natural Magic by Nigel Pennick
The Good Witch's Guide by Shawn Robbins and Charity Bedell
The Way of Shamanism by Leo Rutherford
Chakra for Everyday Living by Liz Simpson and Patricia Mercier
Tantra by Val Simpson
The Magic of Herbs by Ted Smart.
The Witch's Companion by Soraya

Wicca: Charms, Potions and Lore by Nixie Vale
Spirit Animals by Stephanie Iris Weiss
Fortune Telling by Hazel Whitaker

Online Resources

Merriam Webster – https://www.merriam-webster.com/dictionary

Cambridge Dictionary – https://dictionary.cambridge.org/dictionary/english

Gods and Mythological Beings in the Younger Futhark (PDF) by McKinnell, John; Simek, Rudolf; Düwel, Klaus – (2004) http://dro.dur.ac.uk/1053/1/1053.pdf?DDD11+DDC65+dac0hsg

Wikipedia (this was used very sparingly) – https://en.wikipedia.org/wiki/Main_Page

Wikipedia: Classical Elements – https://en.wikipedia.org/wiki/Classical_element

How to Use an Abundance Cheque https://www.linkedin.com/pulse/write-abundance-check-new-moon-susan-fix

The Times of India – Elemental Influence: How Earth, Fire, Wair and Air Signs Shape Personalities – https://timesofindia.indiatimes.com/astrology/zodiacs-astrology/elemental-influence-how-earth-fire-water-and-air-signs-shape-personalities/articleshow/113601125.cms

Britannica – https://www.britannica.com/topic/alchemy I have used Britannica for a number of entries.

Tidal: The Cult of Crowley – https://tidal.com/magazine/article/cult-crowley/1-93413

Learn Religions: Alexandrian Wicca – https://www.learnreligions.com/alexandrian-wicca-2562902 and https://alexandrianwitchcraft.org

Learn Religions: How to Consecrate Magical Tools and Items – https://www.learnreligions.com/consecrate-your-magical-tools-2562860

Learn Religions: The Cone of Power – https://www.learnreligions.com/the-cone-of-power-2561490

Learn Religions: What is a Hedgewitch – https://www.learnreligions.com/hedge-witch-4768392

I use Learn Religions a lot: https://www.learnreligions.com

Wisdom Library https://www.wisdomlib.org/definition/akasha

HelenWoods.com: Beginners Guide to Reading the Akashic Records https://helenawoods.com/beginners-guide-to-reading-the-akashic-records/

Medium.com https://medium.com/holisticism

Palos Verdes Pulse – https://www.palosverdespulse.com/blog/angels

Centre of Excellence – https://www.centreofexcellence.com/what-are-angel-numbers-and-their-meanings/

Internet Encyclopaedia of Philosophy – https://iep.utm.edu/animism/

The Open Encyclopaedia of Anthropology – https://www.anthroencyclopedia.com/entry/animism

Universal Life Church – https://www.ulc.org/ulc-blog/the-purpose-of-anointing

Wikipedia: Anthropomorphism – https://en.wikipedia.org/wiki/Anthropomorphism

Biddy Tarot – https://biddytarot.com

Ascension Glossary – https://ascensionglossary.com/index.php/Ascended_Master

The Quantum Lab – https://www.newworldblueprints.com/what-is-an-ascended-master/

The Magickal Spot – https://magickalspot.com

The Blue Moon Manor – http://www.blue-moon-manor.com

Space.com – https://www.space.com/34162-black-moon-guide.html

Quora.com – https://www.quora.com/What-is-the-definition-of-binding-in-witchcraft

Spooky Scotland – https://spookyscotland.net

Neptunes Daughter – https://www.neptunesdaughter.co.uk/blog/candlemas-or-imbolc/

Teen Vogue: Learn about Cartomancy – https://www.teenvogue.com/story/tarot-with-playing-cards

Chroma Gems – https://chromagems.com/blog/technical/gemstone-asterism/

Her Campus: A Breakdown of Closed and Open Practices Within Spirituality – https://www.hercampus.com/school/cu-boulder/a-breakdown-of-closed-and-open-practices-within-spirituality/

EScolorship.com: Anthropomorphic Deities – https://escholarship.org/uc/item/5s54w4tc

Art of the Root: Dressing and Anointing Candles – https://www.google.com/search?client=firefox-b-d&q=daemon+meaning

51Pyraminds – https://51pyramids.in/pages

Fairytale Apothecary: Types of Fae – https://fairytaleapothecary.com/blogs/fairylore-and-mythical-beings/types-of-fae

Theoi.com – https://www.theoi.com/Daimon/Moirai.html

History.com – https://www.history.com/topics/folklore

Healthline – What are Chakras – https://www.healthline.com/health/what-are-chakras

Healthline – What is an Aura – https://www.healthline.com/health/what-is-an-aura

Forever Consciousness: The 7 Layers of your Aura – https://foreverconscious.com/7-layers-aura

The Real Danielle – The Layers of the Aura https://therealheatherdanielle.com/layers-of-the-aura/

Shondaland – https://www.shondaland.com/live/a36560463/what-is-glam-magic/

Gerald Gardner.com – https://www.geraldgardner.com/

Way of the Witch: Graveyard Dirt – https://www.thewayofwitch.com/graveyard-dirt-for-protection/

Reddit: Grave Dirt vs Graveyard Dirt – https://www.reddit.com/r/witchcraft/comments/feh1fp/grave_dirt_vs_graveyard_dirt/

Tryskelion: Temples, Govens & Groves – https://www.tryskelion.com/art_temples_covens.html

Pagan/Wicca Holy Days Calendar – Office of Religious and Spiritual Life – https://orsl.usc.edu/life/pagan-wicca-holy-days-calendar/

On Curses, Hexes, and Jinxes – Your Friendly Neighbourhood Witch – https://friendlystreetwitch.com/2021/04/22/on-curses-hexes-and-jinxes/

Hermetic Order of the Golden Dawn – Wikipedia – https://en.wikipedia.org/wiki/Hermetic_Order_of_the_Golden_Dawn

Syncretism – Wikipedia – https://en.wikipedia.org/wiki/Syncretism

Witchcraft | Definition, History, Trials, Witch Hunts, & Facts | Britannica – https://www.britannica.com/topic/witchcraft

How to use natural resins and incense mixtures – Rene Schonefeld – https://reneschonefeld.com/blog/how-to-use-incense/

What Is A Spell Jar? – Mercat Tours Ltd, Edinburgh, Scotland – https://www.mercattours.com/blog-post/what-is-a-spell-jar

Reddit: Genie vs Jinn – https://www.reddit.com/r/mythology/comments/179bt24/which_term_do_you_prefer_genie_jinn_or_djinn/

Kemetic Orthodoxy – Wikipedia – https://en.wikipedia.org/wiki/Kemetic_Orthodoxy

Witchcraft 101: Keys — Three Morrigna – https://www.threemorrigna.com/witchy-writings/2019/6/14/witchcraft-101-keys

What Is Knot Magic? | by Pravin M1989 | Medium – https://medium.com/@Pravin1989/what-is-knot-magic-f570af473f50

Lenormand Card Meanings and Combinations List – Labyrinthos – https://labyrinthos.co/blogs/lenormand-cards
Wikipedia: Key of Solomon – https://en.wikipedia.org/wiki/Key_of_Solomon
Lithomancy – Wikipedia – https://en.wikipedia.org/wiki/Lithomancy
Celestial equator – Wikipedia – https://en.wikipedia.org/wiki/Celestial_equator magick | The Pluralism Project – https://pluralism.org/magick
The Maypole – what does it mean and what does it signify? | Articles & stories – https://www.oakhousefoods.co.uk/blog/blog/2019/05/03/the-maypole-what-does-is-it-and-what-does-it-signify/
Cleveland Clinic: Meditation – https://my.clevelandclinic.org/health/articles/17906-meditation
Britannica: Shamanism – https://www.britannica.com/topic/medium-occultism
All Poetry – https://allpoetry.com/poem/7303717-Merry-Meet--Merry-Part--and-Merry-Meet-Again-by-MusicAtMidnight
Learn Religions: Hereditary Witchcraft – https://www.learnreligions.com/about-hereditary-witchcraft-2562544
Time and Date: Hunter's Moon or Harvest Moon – https://www.timeanddate.com/astronomy/moon/hunters.html
NASA – https://science.nasa.gov/solar-system/moons/
Mimisbrunnr.info: Nine Herbs Charm – https://www.mimisbrunnr.info/nigon-wyrta-galdor

MOON BOOKS

PAGANISM & SHAMANISM

What is Paganism? A religion, a spirituality, an alternative belief system, nature worship? You can find support for all these definitions (and many more) in dictionaries, encyclopaedias, and text books of religion, but subscribe to any one and the truth will evade you. Above all Paganism is a creative pursuit, an encounter with reality, an exploration of meaning and an expression of the soul. Druids, Heathens, Wiccans and others, all contribute their insights and literary riches to the Pagan tradition. Moon Books invites you to begin or to deepen your own encounter, right here, right now. If you have enjoyed this book, why not tell other readers by posting a review on your preferred book site.

Bestsellers from Moon Books

Keeping Her Keys
An Introduction to Hekate's Modern Witchcraft
Cyndi Brannen
Blending Hekate, witchcraft and personal development together to create
a powerful new magickal perspective.
Paperback: 978-1-78904-075-3 ebook 978-1-78904-076-0

Journey to the Dark Goddess
How to Return to Your Soul
Jane Meredith
Discover the powerful secrets of the Dark Goddess and transform your depression, grief and pain into healing and integration.
Paperback: 978-1-84694-677-6 ebook: 978-1-78099-223-5

Shamanic Reiki
Expanded Ways of Working with Universal Life Force Energy
Llyn Roberts, Robert Levy
Shamanism and Reiki are each powerful ways of healing; together, their power multiplies. Shamanic Reiki introduces techniques to help healers and Reiki practitioners tap ancient healing wisdom.
Paperback: 978-1-84694-037-8 ebook: 978-1-84694-650-9

Southern Cunning
Folkloric Witchcraft in the American South
Aaron Oberon
Modern witchcraft with a Southern flair, this book is a journey through the folklore of the American South and a look at the power these stories hold for modern witches.
Paperback: 978-1-78904-196-5 ebook: 978-1-78904-197-2

Bestsellers from Moon Books
Pagan Portals Series

The Morrigan

Meeting the Great Queens

Morgan Daimler

Ancient and enigmatic, the Morrigan reaches out to us. On shadowed wings and in raven's call, meet the ancient Irish goddess of war, battle, prophecy, death, sovereignty, and magic.

Paperback: 978-1-78279-833-0 ebook: 978-1-78279-834-7

The Awen Alone

Walking the Path of the Solitary Druid

Joanna van der Hoeven

An introductory guide for the solitary Druid, The Awen Alone will accompany you as you explore, and seek out your own place within the natural world.

Paperback: 978-1-78279-547-6 ebook: 978-1-78279-546-9

Moon Magic

Rachel Patterson

An introduction to working with the phases of the Moon, what they are and how to live in harmony with the lunar year and to utilise all the magical powers it provides.

Paperback: 978-1-78279-281-9 ebook: 978-1-78279-282-6

Hekate

A Devotional

Vivienne Moss

Hekate, Queen of Witches and the Shadow-Lands, haunts the pages of this devotional bringing magic and enchantment into your lives.

Paperback: 978-1-78535-161-7 ebook: 978-1-78535-162-4

Readers of ebooks can buy or view any of these bestsellers by clicking on the live link in the title. Most titles are published in paperback and as an ebook. Paperbacks are available in traditional bookshops. Both print and ebook formats are available online.

For video content, author interviews and more, please subscribe to our YouTube channel.

MoonBooksPublishing

Follow us on social media for book news, promotions and more:

Facebook: Moon Books

Instagram: @MoonBooksCI

Blog: https://thepagancollective.com

TikTok: @MoonBooksCI

What People Are Saying About

Witchitorium

Words have power, they provide us with communication but also work magic. Having an understanding of those words in a magical context is paramount to successful workings. This book gives a very comprehensive guide to terms found within the world of witchcraft, something any new or even more experienced witch will appreciate. A very useful tome of magical wordage!
Rachel Patterson, English Witch and best-selling author with over 30 books published on the subject of witchcraft

Spiritualism is a multi-faceted world of layered understanding and this often causes confusion as to what the terminology means. Nixie Vale has years of experience not just in the practical but also in her knowledge base and has written the ideal handbook which breaks down each term and brings each individual facet to the fore. This is a must have book for all levels of practicing spiritualists to use as a reference which will enhance their journey and eliminate any confusion.
Kerry Greenaway

Witchitorium deserves a place in the library of every witch. Nixie Vale will take you on a wonderful journey through a magickal collection of terms that every witch will come across and want to know on their path. As a witch of well over 20 years, I was excited to spend time with this collection and to learn so many new things. I do believe everyone will find something new that calls to them in *Witchitorium*.
Jasmeine Moonsong, author of *Moonsong Daily Magick*